Twenty-four Hours a Day
for Everyone

Twenty-four
Hours
a Day
for Everyone

compiled by
Alan L. Roeck

Box 176   Center City, MN 55012

The Serenity Prayer

God grant me the serenity
To accept the things I cannot change,
The courage to change the things I can,
And the wisdom to know the difference.

Look to this day,
For it is life,
The very life of life.
In its brief course lie all
The realities and verities of existence,
The bliss of growth,
The splendor of action,
The glory of power—

For yesterday is but a dream
And tomorrow is only a vision.
But today, well lived,
Makes every yesterday a dream
  of happiness
And every tomorrow a vision of hope.

Look well, therefore, to this day.

SANSKRIT PROVERB

Foreword

*T*wenty-four Hours a Day was intended for members of Alcoholics Anonymous, as a help in their program of living one day at a time. This version, *Twenty-four Hours a Day for Everyone*, is an adaptation designed for those suffering from other emotional and spiritual afflictions whose recovery program is modeled after the Twelve Steps and Twelve Traditions of Alcoholics Anonymous. These groups include Al-Anon, Alateen, Emotions Anonymous, Overeaters Anonymous, Narcotics Anonymous, Parents Anonymous, and Emotional Health Anonymous.

These readings will help those who want to start each day with a few minutes of thought, meditation, and prayer.

It is hoped that these daily messages may help the readers find the strength they need to sustain them in their recovery each twenty-four hours and to guide them in the new lives they are building. May they bring to each reading the special brand of miracles their groups are working in their lives.

Twenty-four Hours a Day
for Everyone

JANUARY 1   THOUGHT FOR THE DAY

When I came into this program, was I a desperate person? Did I have a soul-sickness? Was I so sick of myself and my way of living that I couldn't stand looking at myself in a mirror? Was I ready for the program? Was I ready to try anything that would help me to get straightened out and to get over my soul-sickness? *Should I ever forget the condition I was in?*

MEDITATION FOR THE DAY

In the new year, I will live one day at a time. I will make each day one of preparation for better things ahead. I will not dwell on the past or the future, only on the present. I will bury every fear of the future, all thoughts of unkindness and bitterness, all my dislikes, my resentments, my sense of failure, my disappointments in others and in myself, my gloom and despondency. I will leave all these things buried and go forward, in this new year, into a new life.

PRAYER FOR THE DAY

I pray that God, as I understand Him, will guide me one day at a time in the new year. I pray that for each day He will supply the wisdom and the strength that I need.

What makes this program work? The first thing is to have a revulsion against my way of living, myself. Then I must admit I am helpless, that my problem has me licked and I can't do anything about it. The next thing is to honestly want to quit the old life. I must then surrender my life to a Higher Power, putting my problem in His hands and leaving it there. After these things are done, I should attend meetings regularly for fellowship and sharing. I should also try to help others who share my affliction. *Am I doing these things?*

MEDITATION FOR THE DAY

Man is so made that he can carry only the weight of twenty-four hours, no more. If he weights himself down with the years behind and the days ahead, his back breaks. God has promised to help you with the burdens of the day only. If you are foolish enough to gather again that burden of the past and carry it, then indeed you cannot expect God to help you bear it. So forget that which lies behind you and breathe in the blessing of each new day.

PRAYER FOR THE DAY

I pray that I may realize that, for good or bad, past days have ended. I pray that I may face each new day, the coming twenty-four hours, with hope and courage.

When I came into this program, I learned the characteristics of one who has this affliction. Then I applied this knowledge to myself to see if I was so afflicted. When I was convinced that I was, I admitted it openly. Since then, have I been learning to live accordingly? Have I read the books and pamphlets? Have I applied to myself the knowledge gained? Have I admitted openly that the program is intended for me? *Am I ready to admit it at any time when I can be of help?*

MEDITATION FOR THE DAY

I will be renewed and in many ways remade. In this, I need a Higher Power to help me. His spirit will flow through me and in so doing will sweep away all the bitter past. I will take heart. The way will open for me. Each day will unfold something good, as long as I am trying to live the way I believe my Higher Power wants me to live.

PRAYER FOR THE DAY

I pray that I may be taught just as a child would be taught. I pray that I will not question God's plans but will accept them gladly.

JANUARY 4   THOUGHT FOR THE DAY

Have I admitted I am afflicted? Have I swallowed my pride and admitted I am different from those who do not have my affliction? Have I accepted the fact that I must spend the rest of my life without that which causes my repeated suffering? Do I have any more reservations, any idea in the back of my mind that someday I'll be able to indulge that behavior again safely? Am I absolutely honest with myself and others? Have I taken an inventory of myself and admitted the wrong I have done? Am I honest with my friends? *Am I trying to make it up to them for what I was?*

MEDITATION FOR THE DAY

I will believe that fundamentally all is well. Good things will happen to me. I believe that God cares for me and will provide for me. I will not try to plan ahead. I know that the way will unfold, step by step. I will leave tomorrow's burden to Him, because only He is the burden-bearer. He only expects me to carry my one-day's share.

PRAYER FOR THE DAY

I pray that I may not try to carry the burden of the universe on my shoulders. I pray that I may be satisfied to do my share each day.

JANUARY 5   THOUGHT FOR THE DAY

Have I turned to a Higher Power for help? Do I believe that each person I see in this group is a demonstration of God's power to change a human being from the victim of a malady to a restored, useful citizen? Do I believe that this Higher Power can keep me from sliding back into those old habits? Am I living one day at a time? Do I ask the God of my understanding to give me the power to stay safe for each twenty-four hours? *Do I attend meetings regularly, as I know I must?*

MEDITATION FOR THE DAY

I believe that God's presence brings peace and that peace is like a quiet-flowing river, cleansing all irritants away. In these quiet times God will teach me how to rest. I will not be afraid. I will learn how to relax. When I am relaxed, His strength will flow into me. I will be at peace.

PRAYER FOR THE DAY

I pray for that peace which passes all understanding. I pray for that peace which the world can neither give nor take away.

Keeping rational is the most important thing in my life. The most important decision I ever made was my decision to abandon that old life-style. I am convinced that my whole life depends on not taking that first step backward. Nothing in the world is as important to me as my newfound sanity. Everything I have, my whole life, depends on that one thing. *Can I afford ever to forget this, even for one moment?*

MEDITATION FOR THE DAY

I will discipline myself. I will do this disciplining now. I will turn out all useless thoughts. I know that the goodness of my life is a necessary foundation for its usefulness. I will welcome this training, for without it God cannot give me His power. I believe that this power is a mighty one when it is used in the right way.

PRAYER FOR THE DAY

I pray that I may face and accept whatever discipline is necessary. I pray that I may be fit to receive God's power in my life.

JANUARY 7   THOUGHT FOR THE DAY

When temptation comes, as it does sometimes to us all, I will say to myself: "No, my whole life depends on not reverting to that crazy way of things. Nothing in this world can make me do it again." I know that God doesn't want me to fall back, and I won't break my promise to God intentionally. I've given up my right to entertain such madness, and it's not my decision any longer. *Have I made the choice once and for all, so that there is no going back on it?*

MEDITATION FOR THE DAY

In silence comes God's meaning to the heart. No man can judge when it enters his heart: he can only judge by results. God's word is spoken in the secret places of my heart, and in some hour of temptation I find that word, realizing its value for the first time. When I need it, I find it there. "Thy Father, who seeth in secret, shall reward thee openly."

PRAYER FOR THE DAY

I pray that I may see God's meaning in my life. I pray that I may gladly accept what God has to teach me.

Everyone who comes into the program knows from bitter experience that he or she can't relive the old errors. I know that these mistakes have been the cause of all my major troubles or have made them worse. Now that I have found a way out, I will hang onto this program with both hands. Saint Paul once said that nothing in the world, neither powers nor principalities, life nor death, could separate him from the love of God. *Once I have given my affliction to God, should anything in the world separate me from my new peace?*

MEDITATION FOR THE DAY

I know that my life will not be immune from difficulties, but I will have peace even in those times. I know that serenity is the result of faithful trusting acceptance of God's will, even in the midst of difficulties. Saint Paul said, "Our light afflictions, which are but for a moment, work for us a far more exceeding and eternal weight of glory."

PRAYER FOR THE DAY

I pray that I may welcome difficulties. I pray that they may test my strength and build my character.

JANUARY 9   THOUGHT FOR THE DAY

When we were irrational, most of us had no real faith in anything. We may have said that we believed in God, but we didn't act as though we did. We never honestly asked God to help us, and we never really accepted His help. To us faith looked like helplessness. But when we came into this program, we began to have faith in God. And we found that faith gave us the strength we needed to overcome our affliction. *Have I learned that there is strength in faith?*

MEDITATION FOR THE DAY

I will have faith, no matter what may befall me. I will be patient, even in the midst of troubles. I will not fear the strain of life, because I believe that God knows just what I can bear. I will look to the future with confidence. I know that God will not ask me to bear anything that could overcome or destroy me.

PRAYER FOR THE DAY

I pray that I may put this day in the hands of God. I pray for faith, so that nothing will upset me or weaken my determination to stay rational.

In the throes of our malady most of us were full of pride and selfishness. We believed that we could handle our affairs, even though we were making a mess of our lives. We were very stubborn and didn't like to take advice. We resented being told what to do. To us, humility looked like weakness. But when we came into this program, we began to be humble. And we found out that humility gave us the power we needed to overcome the old life-style. *Have I learned that there is power in humility?*

MEDITATION FOR THE DAY

I will come to God in faith, and He will give me a new way of living. This new way will alter my whole existence, the words I speak, the influence I have. They will spring from the life within me. I see how important is the work of a person who has this new way of life. The words and example of such a person can have a wide influence for good in the world.

PRAYER FOR THE DAY

I pray that I may learn the principles of the good life. I pray that I may meditate upon them and work at them because they are eternal.

JANUARY 11   THOUGHT FOR THE DAY

When we were distraught, most of us never thought of helping others. We liked to bend someone's ear, because that made us feel like big shots. But we only used others for our own pleasure. To go out and try to help someone who needed help never occurred to us. To us, helping others looked like a sucker's game. But when we came into this program, we began to try to help others. And we found out that helping others made us happy and also helped us to follow the program. *Have I learned that there is happiness in helping others?*

MEDITATION FOR THE DAY

I will seek to gain strength and find ways to recognize God's will. I will use my Higher Power's unlimited store of strength for my needs, seeking His will for me. I will strive to have conscious awareness of His presence in me, for I now believe that His is the light of the world. I have become yet another pilgrim, with His strength and guidance for this day.

PRAYER FOR THE DAY

I pray that I may seek God's guidance day by day. I pray that I will strive to abide in His presence in this new life.

JANUARY 12 THOUGHT FOR THE DAY

The longer we are in the program, the more natural this way of life seems. Our old, unstable lives were a very unnatural situation. Our present, saner lives are the most natural way we could possibly live. During the early years of our instability, our lives weren't so different from the lives of a lot of other people. But as we gradually grew more dominated by our affliction, our lives became more and more unnatural. *Do I realize now that the things I did were far from natural?*

MEDITATION FOR THE DAY

I will say, "Thank you," to the God of my understanding for everything, even the seeming trials and miseries. I will strive to be grateful and humble, profiting from my suffering. My whole attitude toward the Higher Power will be one of gratitude. I will be glad for the things I have received, and will pass on what He reveals to me. I believe that more truths will flow in as I go along in this new way of living.

PRAYER FOR THE DAY

I pray that I may be grateful for the things I have received and seemed not to deserve. I pray that this gratitude will make me truly humble.

JANUARY 13 THOUGHT FOR THE DAY

When we were "hurting," we were living an un-natural life physically and mentally. Our spirits were dead. We were punishing ourselves in various ways — through drugs, alcohol, crises, food, crutches, and escapes. We ate too little or too much; we slept too much or too little; we abused ourselves or others; and we were ruining ourselves in many ways. Life without our obsession was beyond imagining. Our dreams were nightmares, visions were fantasies, relations with others were paranoid plots. *Since I came into this program, am I getting better?*

MEDITATION FOR THE DAY

I believe that my life is being refined like gold in a crucible. Gold does not stay in the crucible, only until it is refined. I will never despair or be despondent, for I now have friends who long for me to conquer. If I should fail or falter, it would cause pain and disappointment to them. I will keep trying to live a better life.

PRAYER FOR THE DAY

I pray that I may always call on God's strength, while the gold of my life is being refined. I pray that I may see it through, with His help.

When we first came into this program, a rational life seemed strange. We wondered what life could possibly be like without reverting to our past behavior. At first, a rational life seemed unnatural; but the longer we're in the program, the more natural this way of life seems. And now we know that the life we're living—the peace of mind, the fellowship, the faith in God, the help we give each other—is the most natural way we could possibly live. *Do I believe this is the way my Higher Power wants me to live?*

MEDITATION FOR THE DAY

I will learn to overcome myself, because every blow to selfishness is used to shape the real, eternal, unperishable me. As I overcome myself, I gain that power which God releases in my soul. And I too will be victorious. It is not the difficulties of life that I need to conquer so much as my own selfishness.

PRAYER FOR THE DAY

I pray that I may obey God and walk with Him and listen to Him. I pray that I may strive to overcome my own selfishness.

JANUARY 15 THOUGHT FOR THE DAY

This program is a way of life. It is a way of living that we need to learn if we're going to remain free of our affliction. The twelve steps are like guideposts that point the direction in which we must go. But each member of the group must find his own best way of living the program. We don't all do it exactly alike. Whether by quiet times in the morning, by meetings, working with others, spreading the word, we have to learn to live the program. *Have I made this program my regular, natural way of living?*

MEDITATION FOR THE DAY

I will relax and not get tense. I will have no fear, because everything will work out in the end. I will learn soul-balance and poise in a vacillating, changing world. I will claim God's power and use it, because, if I do not use it, that power will be withdrawn. As long as I get back to God and replenish my strength after each task, no work can be too much.

PRAYER FOR THE DAY

I pray that I may relax and that God's strength will be given to me. I pray that I may subject my will to His will and be free of all tenseness.

This program is more a way of building a new life than just a way of getting over a personal affliction. Because in the program we don't just stop the anguish. We did that lots of times in the old days whenever we were unperturbed for a while. And of course we always reverted once again, since we were only waiting for a chance to do so. Once we've got our sanity and perspective back through this program, we start going uphill. In our days of affliction we were going downhill, getting ever worse. We either go down or up. *Am I going uphill, getting better and better?*

MEDITATION FOR THE DAY

I will try to obey God's will day in and day out, in the wilderness plains as well as on the mountaintops of experience. It is in the daily striving that our perseverance counts. I believe that my Higher Power is also Lord of little things. I will persist in this new way of living, since I know that nothing in the day is too small to be a part of His scheme of things.

PRAYER FOR THE DAY

I pray that the little stones that I put into the mosaic of my life will make a worthwhile pattern. I pray that I may persevere and so find harmony and beauty in living.

JANUARY 17   THOUGHT FOR THE DAY

It doesn't do much good to come to meetings only once in a while and sit around, hoping to get something out of the program. That's all right at first, but it won't help us very long. Sooner or later we have to get into action, by coming to meetings regularly, by giving a personal witness of our experiences, and by trying to help other members. Building a new life takes all the energy that we used to spend on our affliction. *Am I spending time and effort on the new life that I'm trying to build through this program?*

MEDITATION FOR THE DAY

I will build a protective screen around myself that will keep out all distracting thoughts. I will fashion it out of my attitude toward the Higher Power and my attitude toward other people. When one worrying or impatient thought enters my mind, I will put it out at once. I know that love and trust are the solvents for the worry and frets of life. These will be a protective screen around me.

PRAYER FOR THE DAY

I pray that impatience and worry may not corrode my protective screen against all evil thoughts. I pray that I may banish all these from my life.

This new life can't be built in a day. We have to take the program slowly, a little at a time. Our subconscious minds have to be re-educated. We have to learn to think differently. We have to get used to coherent thinking instead of chaotic thinking. Anyone who tries it knows that the old distorted thinking is apt to come back when we least expect it. Building a new life is a slow process, but it can be done if we really follow the program. *Am I building a new life on the foundation of rational thinking?*

MEDITATION FOR THE DAY

I will strive daily to build faith. On faith depends my success in rebuilding my life. My Higher Power gives it to me in response to my asking, because it is a necessary weapon for me to use in overcoming all adverse conditions and accomplishing good in my life. Therefore, I will work at strengthening my faith.

PRAYER FOR THE DAY

I pray that I may so think and live as to feed my faith in God. I pray that my faith may grow, because with faith His power becomes available to me.

JANUARY 19 THOUGHT FOR THE DAY

On a foundation of rationality we can build a life of honesty, unselfishness, faith, and love of our fellow human beings. We'll never fully reach these goals, but the adventure of building that kind of life is so much better than the old chaotic life that there is no comparison. We come into this program to ease our affliction, but if we stay long enough, we learn a new way of living. We become honest with ourselves and with others. We learn to put others first. And we learn to rely on the constancy of our Higher Power. *Am I living the way of honesty, unselfishness, and faith?*

MEDITATION FOR THE DAY

I believe that my Higher Power already knew my heart's needs before I cried to Him. I believe that He was preparing the answer. God does not have to be petitioned with sighs and tears and much speaking before He gives the help so desperately needed. He has anticipated my every want and need, which I come to know as His plans unfold in my daily life.

PRAYER FOR THE DAY

I pray that I may understand my real wants and needs. I pray that God will grant me the capacity for honesty, unselfishness, and love.

In this program we're all through with lying, re-morse, deceptions, and wasting money. Before we came into this program, we were only half alive. Now that we're trying to live decent, honest, unselfish lives, we're really alive. This life has new meaning for us so that we can truly enjoy it. We're on the right side of the fence, instead of on it or on the wrong side. We can look the world in the face instead of hiding in alleys or shutting ourselves in. *Am I convinced that, no matter how much fun I got out of the older life, that life never was as good as the one I'm now building?*

MEDITATION FOR THE DAY

I have decided that I will set my deepest affections on things spiritual, not on things material. As a man thinks, so is he. I will think of and desire that which will help, not hinder, my spiritual growth. I will try to be at one with my Higher Power. No human aspiration can reach higher than this.

PRAYER FOR THE DAY

I pray that my despair and despondency are now past. I pray that no false goals will again delude me.

To grasp this program we have to think things out. Saint Paul said, "They are transformed by the renewing of their minds." We have to learn to think straight. We have to change from addictive, obsessive, compulsive thinking to sober, sane, rational thinking. We must build a new way of looking at life. Before we came into this program, we wanted an artificial life of excitement, thrills, escape—whatever goes with the insanity of our affliction. That kind of life looked normal to us then. But now that life looks the exact opposite of normal. We must re-educate our minds. *Am I changing from an abnormal thinker to a normal, rational thinker?*

MEDITATION FOR THE DAY

I will live the most crowded day without fear. I believe that God is with me and controlling all. I will let confidence be the motif running through all the crowded day. I will not be worried, because I know that God is my helper. Underneath are the everlasting arms. I will rest in them, even though the day be full of things crowding in upon me.

PRAYER FOR THE DAY

I pray that I may be calm and let nothing upset me. I pray that I may not let material things control me and choke out spiritual things.

In the beginning, you want to overcome your malady, but you're helpless, and so you turn to a Power greater than yourself. By trusting in that Higher Power, you get the strength to arrest the affliction. From then on you want to keep control, and that's a matter of re-educating your mind. After a while you come to really enjoy simple, healthy, normal living. You get a kick out of life without the warps of distress. All you have to do is look around at the members of the group, and you will see how their outlook has changed. *Is my outlook on life changing?*

MEDITATION FOR THE DAY

I will never forget to say, "Thank you," to God, even on the grayest days. My attitude will be one of humility and gratitude. Saying, "Thank you," to God is a daily practice that is absolutely necessary. If a day is not one of thankfulness, the practice has to be repeated until it becomes so. Gratitude is a necessity for those who seek to live a better life.

PRAYER FOR THE DAY

I pray that gratitude will bring humility. I pray that humility will bring me to a better life.

The affliction of distressed, tormented people has led them down a blind alley. They have not been able to learn from chaotic experiences. They make the same mistakes and suffer the same consequences over and over again. They cannot admit that they have the affliction, still believing that they can "manage" it. Pride and refusals keep them from acknowledging that they are different from ordinary people. They won't face the fact that they must spend the rest of their lives without further indulgence. They can't visualize life without that behavior. *Am I out of this blind alley?*

MEDITATION FOR THE DAY

I believe that the God of my understanding has all power. It is His to give, His to withhold. But He will not withhold it from those who dwell near Him. It is breathed in by those who live in His presence. By so living, I will have the things I desire of Him— strength, power, and joy. God's power is available to all who need it and are willing to accept it.

PRAYER FOR THE DAY

I pray that I may no longer be blind and that God's power will allow me to see. I pray that I may surrender myself to that power.

Harrowed people who are living in a blind alley refuse to be really honest with themselves or with
others. They are running away from life and won't
face things as they are. They won't give up their resentments. They are too sensitive and too easily hurt.
They refuse to try to be unselfish. They want everything for themselves. No matter how many disastrous experiences they have had with their deluded
behavior, they still repeat it over and over again.
There is only one way to escape the blind alley, and
that is to change one's thinking. *Have I changed my
thinking?*

MEDITATION FOR THE DAY

I know that the vision and power that I receive from
my Higher Power are limitless, as far as spiritual
things are concerned. But in temporal and material
things I must submit to limitations. I know that I cannot see the road ahead. I must go just one step at a
time, because He does not grant me a longer view. I
am in uncharted territory, limited by my temporal
and spatial life, but unlimited in my spiritual life.

PRAYER FOR THE DAY

I pray that, in spite of my material limitations, I may
follow God's way. I pray that I may learn that trying
to do His will is perfect freedom.

We used to depend on drugs, alcohol, a feast, a "kick" from odds, an emotional explosion—all these for a lot of reasons. We depended on them for a lift, to help us enjoy things. They broke down our shyness or gave us relief or kept the world from caving in. We depended on them to help us when we felt low. If we later had remorse, a hangover, nausea, we still went back to them. We used them to "counteract" a fight or a bad day at work or when things went against us for no known reason. We always felt better after a shot, a few drinks, a spending spree, an eating binge, a beating up. It got so we depended on them for almost anything. *Have I got over that dependence on "kicks"?*

MEDITATION FOR THE DAY

I believe that complete surrender of my life to God is the foundation of serenity. God has prepared for us many mansions. I do not look upon that promise as referring only to the afterlife. I do not look upon this life as something to be struggled through in order to get the rewards of the next life. I believe that the Kingdom of God is within us and that we can enjoy eternal life here and now.

PRAYER FOR THE DAY

I pray that I may try to do God's will. I pray that such understanding, vision, and insight will be mine as will make my life eternal, here and now.

As we became distraught, the bad effects of our affliction came more and more to outweigh the good effects. But the strange part of it is that, no matter what
our problems did to us—loss of our health, our jobs,
our money, and our homes—we still stuck to our
sickness and depended on it. Our dependence on it
became an obsession. In this program we find a new
outlook. We learn how to change from irrational
thinking to rational thinking. And we find that we
can no longer depend on that affliction for anything.
We depend on a Higher Power instead. *Have I entirely
given up that dependence on my affliction?*

MEDITATION FOR THE DAY

I will try to keep my life calm and unruffled. This is
my great task: to find peace and acquire serenity. I
must not harbor disturbing thoughts. No matter what
fears, worries, and resentments I may have, I must
try to think of constructive things until calmness
comes. Only when I am calm can I act as a channel for
God's spirit.

PRAYER FOR THE DAY

I pray that I may build up instead of tearing down. I
pray that I may be constructive and not destructive.

Obsessed people carry an awful load around with them. What a load lying puts on our shoulders! Drinking, getting high, unleashing emotions, gambling, gorging make liars out of all of us. In order to get the stimuli we want, we have to lie all the time. We have to lie about where we've been, what we've done. When we are lying, we are only half alive, because of the constant fear of being discovered. When we come into this program and get honest with ourselves and with others, that terrible load falls off our shoulders. *Have I got rid of that load of lying?*

MEDITATION FOR THE DAY

I believe that in the spiritual world, as in the material world, there is no empty space. As fears and worries depart from my life, the things of the spirit come in to take their place. Calm comes after a storm. As soon as I am rid of fears and hates and selfishness, God's love and peace can come in.

PRAYER FOR THE DAY

I pray that I may rid myself of all fears and resentments so that peace and serenity may take their place. I pray that I may sweep my life clean of evil so that good may come in.

THOUGHT FOR THE DAY

What a load our affliction puts on our shoulders! What terrible physical and mental punishment we've all been through. The headaches, jumpy nerves, shakes, sweats, knotted stomachs, hallucinations! When we come into this program and halt the sickness, that terrible load of miseries falls from our shoulders. That terrible agony we've all been through. The shame for the things we've said and done. The fear of facing people because of what they might think or say. The fear of the consequences of what we did when we were so obsessed. What a beating the mind takes! When we come into this program, that load of remorse is lifted. *Have I got rid of all these burdens of remorse?*

MEDITATION FOR THE DAY

When we seek to follow this program, we are also seeking to follow the way of the spirit. This often means a complete reversal of the way of the world that we have previously followed. But it is a reversal that leads to happiness and peace. Do the aims and ambitions that we usually strive to achieve bring peace? Do the world's awards bring inner rest and happiness? Or do they turn to ashes in the mouth after a time?

PRAYER FOR THE DAY

I pray that I may not be weary, disillusioned, or disappointed. I pray that I may put my trust not in the ways of the world but in the way of the spirit.

What a burden wasting money puts on our shoulders! They say that our members have paid extremely high initiation fees because we've wasted so much money on our excesses. We'll never be able to figure out how much it was. We wasted not only our own money but also money we should have spent on our families and money others spent on us. When we come into this program, that terrible load of waste falls from our shoulders. We were getting round-shouldered from carrying all these loads. But when we accept the steps and traditions, we get a wonderful new feeling of release and freedom. *Can I throw back my shoulders and look the world in the face again?*

MEDITATION FOR THE DAY

I am no longer at the mercy of my affliction or buffeted about by life. I am being led in a very definite way, as I try to rebuild my life. I believe that the future is in the hands of my Higher Power, Who knows better than I what the future holds for me. I am the builder, but He is the Architect. My life is mine to build as best I can, but under His guidance.

PRAYER FOR THE DAY

I pray that I may depend on God, since He has planned my life. I pray that all the waste is over, that my shoulders are freed of their burden, and that I may live my life as God wants me to live it.

The life we lead as a result of our affliction isn't a happy life. It cuts us off from other people and from God. One of the worst things about it is the eventual loneliness. And one of the best things about this program is the fellowship. This tormenting malady cuts us off from other people, at least those who matter most to us, our families, our co-workers, our close friends. No matter how much we love each one, we build up a wall by our distress. This cuts us off from any real companionship with them. As a result, we are terribly lonely. *Have I got rid of my loneliness?*

MEDITATION FOR THE DAY

I will sometimes go aside into a quiet place of retreat with God. In that place I will find restoration and healing. I will plan quiet times now and then, when I will commune with the God of my understanding and return rested and refreshed. I know that He will never give me a load greater than I can bear. It is in serenity and peace that all true success lies.

PRAYER FOR THE DAY

I pray that I may strengthen my inner life so that I will find serenity. I pray that my soul will be restored in quietness and peace.

Our affliction cuts us off from God and others. No matter how we were brought up, or what our religion is, or if we profess a belief in God, we build an invisible wall between us and God by our excesses. We know that we're not living the way He wants us to live. As a result, we have that terrible, persistent remorse. When we come to meetings, we begin to get right with our Higher Power and with others. A rational life is a happy one, because, by giving up liquor, drugs, abuses, obsessions, compulsions, we get rid of remorse and then loneliness. *Do I have real fellowship with God and with others?*

MEDITATION FOR THE DAY

I believe that all sacrifice and all suffering are of some value to me. When I am in pain, I am being tested. Can I trust in the Higher Power, no matter how low I feel? Can I say, "Thy will be done," no matter how much I am defeated? If I can, my faith is real, for it works in the bad times as well as in the good times. My Higher Power is working in a way that is beyond my finite mind to understand, but I can still trust in Him.

PRAYER FOR THE DAY

I pray that I may take my suffering in stride. I pray that I may accept pain and defeat as part of God's plan for my spiritual growth.

FEBRUARY 1   THOUGHT FOR THE DAY

When we consider returning to the excesses of our past, we're thinking of the thrill we get, the pleasure, the escape, the release, the feeling of self-importance, the companionship of others who join us. What we don't think about is the letdown, the remorse, the waste, and the facing of another day. In other words, when we think about that excess, we're thinking of the assets, not of the liabilities. What has the sickness got that we haven't replaced in this program? *Do I believe that the liabilities of excesses outweigh the assets?*

MEDITATION FOR THE DAY

I will start a new life each day. I will put the old mistakes away and start anew each day. My Higher Power always offers me a fresh start. I will not be burdened or anxious. If His forgiveness were only for the righteous and nonsinners, where would be its need? I believe that God forgives us if we are honestly trying to live today the way He wants us to live. Do we forgive ourselves?

PRAYER FOR THE DAY

I pray that my life may not be spoiled by worry or fear or selfishness. I pray that I may have a glad, thankful, and humble heart.

FEBRUARY 2   THOUGHT FOR THE DAY

At first we got a kind of boost from our affliction, before we were overwhelmed by it. For a while the world seemed to look brighter, more exciting. But how about the letdown, the painful aftermath? In this program we get a real boost, not a false feeling of exhilaration but a genuine feeling of satisfaction with ourselves and a new self-respect. And we have a feeling of friendliness toward the world that is not like the sick pleasures of before. Then we thought that we were happy, but it was an illusion. *Am I getting real pleasure and serenity from this program?*

MEDITATION FOR THE DAY

I will practice love, because lack of love will block the way. I will try to see good in all others, those I like and also those who bother me. They are all children of God. If I don't give love, how can I dwell in His spirit, from which nothing unloving can come? I will try to get along with all people, because the more love I give away, the more I will have.

PRAYER FOR THE DAY

I pray that I may do all I can to love others, in spite of their faults. I pray that as I love so will I be loved.

Through our sick behavior we escaped from boredom for a while. We almost forgot our troubles. But when we came to our senses, our troubles were twice as bad. In this program we really do escape boredom. No one is bored at a meeting. We stay on after it's over, and we go home reluctantly. Our distresses gave us a temporary feeling of importance. When we were like that, we kidded ourselves into thinking we were really something else. We told tall tales to build ourselves up. Here we don't want that kind of self-importance. We have found real self-respect, honesty, and humility. *Have I found something much better and more satisfactory than the old life?*

MEDITATION FOR THE DAY

I believe that having a faith and turning my problems over to a Higher Power can accomplish anything in human relationships. There is no limit to what these two things can do for me. Only believe, and anything can happen. Saint Paul said, "I can do all things through Him who strengtheneth me." All walls that divide me from other beings can fall by my faith and God's power. These are the two essentials. All people can be moved by them.

PRAYER FOR THE DAY

I pray that I may try to strengthen my faith day by day. I pray that I may rely more and more on God's power.

FEBRUARY 4   THOUGHT FOR THE DAY

Talking with others about our excessive ways gave us a sick ego trip that was satisfying. We liked to say, "I know what you mean!" But we were not really doing them a favor, but only helping to foster self-pity and encouraging destructive behavior. In this program we really try to help others. We build them up instead of tearing them down. Before, sharing our miseries created a sort of fellowship, based on selfish indulgence and a need to tell others about it. Here we have real fellowship, based on unselfishness and a desire to help each other. And we make real friends, not fair-weather friends. *With a new perspective, have I got everything that the old excesses gave me, but without the old miseries that came later?*

MEDITATION FOR THE DAY

I know that God cannot teach anyone who is trusting in a crutch. When I throw away the crutch and the self-pity and walk with my Higher Power, I find that I am so invigorated that it is simplicity itself. There is never a limit to the power of faith. I will go on to victory one step at a time, one day at a time. There is no profound cure overnight. As in the rest of life, nothing worth having is likely to come quickly. Patience will hasten the victory.

PRAYER FOR THE DAY

I pray that I may have more faith and more dependence on God. I pray that His power may replace the crutch I thought I needed.

One thing we learn in this program is to take a long view of our affliction instead of a short view. When we were bereft of sense, we thought more about the pleasure or release that our outburst would give us than we did about the consequences. This kind of chaos looked good from the short view. When we watch TV, we see life dressed up in distorted trappings, unreal, phony. It looks great, but it isn't real. *Have I learned that what is inside and behind that artificial pleasure is just plain poison to me?*

MEDITATION FOR THE DAY

I believe that life is a kind of school in which I must learn spiritual things. I must trust in my Higher Power and let Him speak through my mind. I must commune with Him in spite of all opposition and every obstacle. There will be days when I will hear no voice in my mind and when there will be no communion. But if I persist and make a life habit of schooling myself in spiritual things, God will reveal Himself to me in many ways.

PRAYER FOR THE DAY

I pray that I may regularly go to school in things of the spirit. I pray that I may grow spiritually, by making a practice of this search.

FEBRUARY 6   THOUGHT FOR THE DAY

On a dark, cool night the gaiety and laughter of the night spots look mighty inviting. Inside there seems to be warmth and good cheer, marvelous food, a lively band. It all looks so inviting, but to some it is the doorway to hell. The expense doesn't end there, nor the misery. And you should see what such a place looks like the morning after. We must also think about what we are like the morning after. *Can I now look straight through the night before?*

MEDITATION FOR THE DAY

At times there is a longing in our hearts for a genuine relationship, one that is not tainted by worldly cynicism, cruel indifference, nor wicked deceitfulness. We think of this as beyond our grasp, but that longing is fulfilled when we awaken to our newfound faith in a Higher Power. We soon learn that love is not betrayed, God is life, and love is His Divine Purpose. Our awakening begins with accepting Him.

PRAYER FOR THE DAY

I pray that I may have a listening ear so that God may speak to me. I pray that I may have a waiting heart so that He may come to me and show me love.

FEBRUARY 7   THOUGHT FOR THE DAY

The visiting area of a hospital or rehabilitation center is often crowded with people all dressed up and patients chatting. It seems to have a warm atmosphere. But you should see the locked wards. What a mass of human suffering. For them the "high" eventually led to a hopeless "low," which is what we so often come to realize about our affliction. We learn to take a long view of this suffering and to think less about the pleasure and more about the low afterward. *Does the high now seem less significant to me and the low afterward more important?*

MEDITATION FOR THE DAY

Only a few more steps and then the Higher Power will make Himself known in my life. That is the promise we are encouraged to accept when we first enter this program. Initially, I was walking in darkness, hearing the entreating voices, the assurance that faith would come, the darkness would be lighted. Groping as I did, I was touched by His power to see, and my cries of anguish were stilled. Hear it from me, those of you who doubt in your darkness. It will come to you if you will it.

PRAYER FOR THE DAY

I pray that the power of God will help strengthen my human weakness. I pray that my pleading will echo through the darkness to the ear of God.

When the morning sun comes up and we jump out of bed, we're so thankful that we feel good instead of sick and disgusted. Serenity and happiness have become much more the day's routine than the excitation of trauma and distress, which lifted us high only to let us fall to greater depths. Of course, all of us had a lot of emotional thrills with our sickness. We might as well admit it, since otherwise it would have never occurred a second time. We can look back on times of excitement, before we grew disoriented by them. But the time comes for all of us when they cease to be any sort of fun and become unadulterated misery. *Have I learned that such excitement can never again be anything but trouble for me?*

MEDITATION FOR THE DAY

I must rely on the Higher Power. I must trust in Him to the limit. I must depend on Him in all human relationships. I will wait and trust and hope. I will meet the test of waiting. I will wait until a thing seems right before I do it. I will seek guidance on each important decision. I know the guidance will come, if I wait for it.

PRAYER FOR THE DAY

I pray that I may meet the test of waiting for God's guidance. I pray that I will have trust and patience.

In the past, we kept right on indulging our excesses in spite of all the trouble we got into. We were foolish enough to believe that they could still be fun in spite of everything that happened to us. When we came into this program, we found a lot of people who, like ourselves, had had fun with this madness but who now admitted that such a life had become nothing but misery for them. And when we found that this had happened to them, too, we realized that we weren't all that odd after all. *Have I admitted that for me these excesses have ceased to be rewarding and have become nothing but trouble?*

MEDITATION FOR THE DAY

The lifeline, the line of rescue, is the line from the soul to our Higher Power. On one end is our faith, and on the other is God's power. It can be a strong line in that no soul can be overwhelmed who is linked to Him. I will trust in this lifeline and never be afraid. God will save me from wrongdoing and from the cares and troubles of life. I will look to Him for help, trusting Him for aid when I am distraught.

PRAYER FOR THE DAY

I pray that no lack of trust or fearfulness will make me disloyal to God. I pray that I may keep a strong hold on the lifeline of faith.

FEBRUARY 10   THOUGHT FOR THE DAY

Since I realized that I had become afflicted and could never have any more involvement with the excesses I had indulged in, and since I knew that more encounters would always get me into more trouble, I realized that the only thing left for me was to stop completely. In this program I learned that I could rely on a Higher Power to help me achieve this goal. I realized that I could work with the Divine Principle in the universe to help me live a sane, useful life. Now I no longer care about not being able to seek old thrills. *Have I learned that I am much happier without them?*

MEDITATION FOR THE DAY

Like a tree, I must be pruned of a lot of dead branches before I will be ready to bear good fruit. Think of changed people as trees that have been stripped of their old branches, pruned, cut and bare. But through the dark, seemingly dead branches flows secretly and silently the new sap, until with the sun of spring comes new life. There are new leaves, buds, blossoms, and fruit many times better because of the pruning. Remember, I am in the hands of a Master Gardener, Who makes no mistakes in His pruning.

PRAYER FOR THE DAY

I pray that I may cut away the deadwood of my life. I pray that I may not mind the pruning, since it helps me to bear good fruit later.

If we're going to stay rational, we've got to learn to want something else more than we want our affliction. When we first came into this program, we couldn't imagine wanting anything but a return to that old pattern. So we had to stop the madness on faith, on faith that someday we really would want something else. But after we've been in the program for a while, we learn that a rational life can really be enjoyed. We learn how nice it is to get along well with our families, to get along at work, to be able to get outside ourselves by helping others. *Have I found that when I stay rational everything else goes well for me?*

MEDITATION FOR THE DAY

There is almost no work in life as hard as waiting. And yet my Higher Power wants me to wait. All motion is easier than calm waiting, and yet I must wait until He shows me His will. So many people have marred their work and hindered the growth of their spiritual lives by too much activity. If I wait patiently, preparing myself always, I will be one day at the place where I want to be. Much impatient activity could not accomplish this so soon.

PRAYER FOR THE DAY

I pray that I may wait patiently. I pray that I may trust God and keep preparing myself for a better life.

FEBRUARY 12   THOUGHT FOR THE DAY

As we look back on all those troubles we used to have when we were out of our minds with our afflictions —the hospitals, the jails, the hearings, the warnings —we wonder why we could have wanted that sort of life at all. As we look back on it, we see that sick life as it really was, and we're glad we're out of it. After a few months in this program we find that we can honestly say that we want something else more than that former chaos. We have learned by experience that a sensible life is really enjoyable, and we wouldn't go back to the other way for anything in this world. *Do I want to stay rational a lot more than I want to be miserable?*

MEDITATION FOR THE DAY

My spiritual life depends on an inner consciousness of a Higher Power. I must be led in all things by my consciousness of God, and I must trust Him in all things. My consciousness of God will always bring peace to me. I will have no fear, because a good future lies before me as long as I keep my consciousness of God. If in every single happening, event, and plan I am conscious of Him, then, no matter what happens, I will be safe in His hands.

PRAYER FOR THE DAY

I pray that I may have this ever-consciousness of God. I pray that I may have a new and better life through this consciousness.

Sometimes we can't help thinking, "Why can't we ever indulge our excesses again?" We know it's because we are powerless over them, but why did we have to get that way? The answer is that at some time in our irrational careers we passed what is called our "tolerance point." When we passed this point, we moved from a condition in which we could tolerate temporary distress to a condition in which we could not tolerate it at all. After that, if we took one slight step in that direction, we would sooner or later go the whole route. *When I think of irrationality now, do I think of it as something that I can never tolerate again?*

MEDITATION FOR THE DAY

In a race, it is when the goal is in sight that heart and nerves and muscles and courage are strained almost to the breaking point. So with us. The goal of the spiritual life is in sight. All we need is the final effort. The saddest records are made by those who run well with brave, stout hearts until the sight of the goal is obliterated by some weakness or self-indulgence. They never know how near they were to the goal and victory.

PRAYER FOR THE DAY

I pray that I may press on until the goal is reached. I pray that I may not lose sight of the goal.

FEBRUARY 14   THOUGHT FOR THE DAY

After that first real encounter with our affliction we had a single-track mind. It was like a missile. Ignition started it off, and it ran its unerring course to where it crashed. We knew that this would happen, but we couldn't keep from trying again. Our will power was gone. We had become helpless and hopeless before the power of irrationality. It's not the second outburst or the tenth that does the damage. It's the first. *Will I ever take that first step to irrationality again?*

MEDITATION FOR THE DAY

I must keep a time apart with God every day. Gradually I will be transformed mentally and spiritually. It is not in the praying alone but, as in these meditation moments, just being in His presence that things work themselves out. The curative powers of this I cannot pretend to understand, because it is His work, not mine. I know that this sick world would be cured if every day each of us sat before God for the inspiration to live as He would have us live.

PRAYER FOR THE DAY

I pray that I may faithfully keep a quiet time apart with God. I pray that through that time I may grow spiritually each day.

If some of our ailments were just a physical condition, like asthma or an allergy, it would be easy for us, by taking a skin test, to find out whether we have it. But our afflictions are not like most allergies. After we've become enslaved by them we can still tolerate it for a while, although we suffer more after each incident. Each time it takes a little longer to get over it. Finally we cannot tolerate these incidents at all. *Since I entered this program, have I accepted that I cannot tolerate these incidents at all?*

MEDITATION FOR THE DAY

The world does not need supermen or superwomen but supernatural people, who will persistently turn the self out of their lives and let the Higher Power work through them. Let inspiration take the place of aspiration. Seek to grow spiritually rather than to acquire fame and riches. Our chief ambition should be to be instruments of the Divine Power. With us as His instruments He can remake the world.

PRAYER FOR THE DAY

I pray that I may be an instrument of the Divine Power. I pray that I may do my share in remaking the world.

FEBRUARY 16 THOUGHT FOR THE DAY

One emotional crisis started a train of thought that became an obsession, and from then on we could not stop the progression. We developed a compulsion to keep repeating the behavior until it was habitual. People generally make two mistakes about this condition. One is believing that it can be cured by physical treatment of some kind. The other mistake is believing that it can be resolved by will power alone. Most of us have tried both and found that they don't work. But in this group we have found a way to arrest our afflictions. *Am I recovering from my affliction by following this program?*

MEDITATION FOR THE DAY

I will try to be unruffled, no matter what happens. I will keep my emotions in check, although others about me are letting theirs go. I will keep calm in the face of disturbances, keep that deep, inner calm through all the experiences of the day. In the rush of work and worry the deep, inner silence is necessary to keep me on an even keel. I must learn to take the calm with me into the most hectic days.

PRAYER FOR THE DAY

I pray that I may be still and commune with God. I pray that I may learn patience, humility, and peace through love.

Mind-changing chemicals are poison to the addict. Mind-changing moods are just as deadly to others. Emotional poisons lead eventually to just as drastic consequences. Death can be quick or slow. On TV these things are all dressed up to make them seem desirable. Even when they are portrayed as "bad," we are told, "But you'll like it!" We should always make it a point to tell ourselves that TV is not reality and that such things are disastrous for us. Overindulgence of any kind has the effect of poisoning our lives. *Do I know that, since I am powerless over my affliction, all such thrills are my enemies?*

MEDITATION FOR THE DAY

I must somehow find the means of coming nearer to my Higher Power. That is what really matters. I must somehow seek the kind of life that assures greater communication with Him. I must grasp at the truth, since all forms of worship lead to this. I must recognize that the negative, lukewarm approach of others is often reluctant pleading for what I have now found through meditation. Do they know that it is theirs, too, for the asking?

PRAYER FOR THE DAY

I pray that I may meet God in quiet communion. I pray that I may share with Him my innermost feelings.

After I became afflicted, that burden poisoned my love for my family, my ambition, my self-respect. It poisoned my whole life, until I came into this group and its program. My life is happier now that it has been redirected. I don't want any drastic event to mar my life. So with the help of my Higher Power and this program I won't take any more of that distress into my life. I'll retrain my mind never to think or react through drugs, alcohol, escapism, obsession. *Do I believe that excesses will poison my life if I ever indulge them again?*

MEDITATION FOR THE DAY

I will liken my frailty to the dust in the tornado. In this affliction I have been blown to the ends of misery and back. Yet I know that the Divine Power stills that wind and knows that I am here. It is not the passionate appeal that gains the Divine attention as much as the silent placing of my difficulty in His hands. So I will trust God to know where I am and to direct me if I but ask. God is pleased more by our trusting confidence than by our pleading cries for help.

PRAYER FOR THE DAY

I pray that I may put all my difficulties in God's hands and leave them there. I pray that I may fully trust Him to take care of them.

Many things we do in this program are in preparation for that crucial time when we're confronted with the same set of circumstances that used to cause us to lapse into our old behavior. It could be any of a variety of things, from an accidental meeting to a planned occasion. If we've trained our minds to be prepared for that crucial event, we won't take the first step. We won't make that tragic slip that has been our undoing so often in the past. There is no guarantee that this will be enough, but it certainly reduces the hazard greatly. *Will I keep my mind on the fact that sooner or later I'll be faced with this challenge again?*

MEDITATION FOR THE DAY

How many of the world's prayers have gone unanswered because those who prayed did not endure to the end? They thought that it was too late and they must act for themselves because God would not guide them. Can I endure to the very end? If so, I will be saved. Endurance requires courage and conviction. If I endure, God will unlock those secret spiritual treasures that are hidden from those who do not endure to the end.

PRAYER FOR THE DAY

I pray that I may follow God's guidance, so that I will endure. I pray that I may never doubt the power of God and take things into my own hands.

Emotionalism used to be my friend, and I used to have a lot of fun toying with emotions. Practically all the fun I had was connected with exploiting them in others if not in myself. But the time came when that turned into a part of my affliction. I don't know just when that happened, but it turned into something no longer fun, and I began to get into trouble. My behavior ceased to be fun, and negative emotionalism became my enemy. My primary concern now is to get things back to a rational level, since my emotions go on as long as I do. *Do I realize that my main concern is to be rational?*

MEDITATION FOR THE DAY

I can depend on a Higher Power to supply me with all the power I need to face any situation, provided I sincerely believe in that power and honestly ask for it. I must also make all my life conform to what I believe God wants it to be. I can address God as an employee does his superior, if I wish. I can lay the matter before Him, get immediate cooperation and relief, if the matter has merit. God and I are able to work it out, no matter what the problem.

PRAYER FOR THE DAY

I pray that I may believe that God is ready and willing to supply me with all that I need in life. I pray that I may ask only for faith and the strength to meet any situation.

I go to the group meetings because it helps me to stay rational about things. And I try to help others when I can, because that is also part of staying rational. As long as I keep in mind that the past excesses are now destructive to me, things are all right. If I can remember that my biggest responsibility is to stay cool and collected, my life is safe. I believe then that I'll be prepared for the crucial moment when the idea of flirting with insanity crosses my mind. *When that idea comes, will I be able to stay rational?*

MEDITATION FOR THE DAY

I will be more afraid of spirit unrest and a ruffled mind than of earthquake or fire. When I feel that the calm of my spirit is broken by emotional upset, then I must be alone with God until I am strong and calm again. Troubled times are the times when evil gains entrance. I will be wary of unguarded moments of unrest. I will try to stay calm, no matter what turmoil surrounds me.

PRAYER FOR THE DAY

I pray that no emotional upheavals will hinder God's power in my life. I pray that I may be of calm spirit and steady heart.

FEBRUARY 22   THOUGHT FOR THE DAY

Now we can take an inventory of the good things that have come to us through this program. To begin with, we're rational today. That's the biggest asset on anyone's books. Tranquillity to us is like good will to a business. Everything else depends on it. Most of us have jobs, which we owe partly to our rationality. We know that we couldn't hold jobs if we were irrational. Most of us have families that we either lost or might have lost if we hadn't stopped our irrational behavior. We have friends in the group who are always ready to help us. *Do I realize that my job, my family, my real friendships are dependent upon my rationality?*

MEDITATION FOR THE DAY

I must trust my Higher Power to the best of my ability. This lesson has to be learned. My doubts and fears continually drive me back into the wilderness. Doubts lead me astray because I am not trusting God. God's love will never fail me, but I must learn not to renounce it by doubt and fear. We all have much to learn in turning out fear by faith. Without faith God's work through us is arrested. Hence I must not doubt. I must believe in Him and continually work to strengthen my faith.

PRAYER FOR THE DAY

I pray that I may live the way God wants me to live. I pray that I may get into the stream of goodness in the world.

Besides our jobs, our families, our friends, and our rationality we have something else that many of us found through this program. That is faith in a Power greater than ourselves to whom we turn for help. There have been many days in the past when we might have taken an inventory and found ourselves very much in the red. We'd have had no job, family, friends, or faith in a Higher Power. Now we have them because He restored our sanity. *Do I make one resolution every day of my life—to stay rational?*

MEDITATION FOR THE DAY

Love the busy life. It is a joy-filled experience. Take your fill of the newness of spring. Live outdoors whenever possible. Sun and air are nature's great healing forces. There is no quicker way to re-establish a receptive attitude than to be surrounded by nature's splendors. As surely as the earth is reborn with the sun's warmth after winter chills, so the spirit is kindled by communion with God's miracle of another springtime. The winter thaw within us is no less profound than that we see all around.

PRAYER FOR THE DAY

I pray that I may learn to live in the springtime of life. I pray that I may enjoy a closer contact with God and watch the flowering of my life continue.

FEBRUARY 24   THOUGHT FOR THE DAY

When we came to our first meeting, we looked up at
the wall at the end of the room and saw the sign "But
for the Grace of God." We knew then that we would
have to call on the grace of God to get over our affliction and become rational again. We heard speakers
tell how they had come to depend on a Power greater
than themselves. That made sense to us, and we
made up our minds to try it. *Am I depending on the
grace of God to help me stay rational?*

MEDITATION FOR THE DAY

Share your love, your joy, your happiness, your time,
your food, your money gladly with all. Give out all
the love you can with a glad, free heart and hand. Do
all you can for others, and in return will come such
countless blessings. Sharing draws others to you. Receive all who come as sent by God. You may never
see the results of your sharing, for today they may
not need you. But tomorrow may bring results from
the sharing of yesterday and today—possibly also
for you.

PRAYER FOR THE DAY

I pray that I may make each visitor desire to return. I
pray that I may never make anyone feel repulsed or
unwanted.

Some people find it hard to believe in a Power greater than themselves. But not to believe in such a Power forces us to be agnostic or atheistic. It has been said that atheism is blind faith in the proposition that this universe originated in a cipher and aimlessly rushes nowhere. That's practically impossible to believe. We can all agree that our affliction is a power greater than ourselves. I was helpless before this power. *Do I remember things that happened to me because of the power of irrationality?*

MEDITATION FOR THE DAY

The spiritual and moral will eventually overcome the material and immoral. Perhaps it will not occur in our lifetime, but that is the purpose and destiny of the human race. Faith, fellowship, and service are cures for most of the ills of the world. There is nothing in personal relationships that they cannot overcome. Our personal encounters are not an adequate test of the eventual outcome, and we must not lose hope.

PRAYER FOR THE DAY

I pray that I may do my share in making a better world. I pray that I may be part of the cure for the ills of that world.

When we came into this program, we came to believe in a Power greater than ourselves. We came to believe that He would offer us the help we needed. So each morning we ask Him for the power to live through the next twenty-four hours. And each night we thank Him for having seen us safely through another day. Each man and woman that I see within this program is living proof of the power of God to change us into rational, worthwhile people. *Do I believe that now I am a rational, worthwhile human being?*

MEDITATION FOR THE DAY

There is nothing lacking in my life now, because all I need is mine. If I lack the faith to know it, then I am like a king's son who sits in rags amidst stores of all things he could desire. Do I know what it means to feel certain that God will never fail me? I must be as certain of this as I am that I breathe. But I still pray for more faith, just as a thirsty traveler prays for water in the desert.

PRAYER FOR THE DAY

I pray for the realization that God has everything I need. I pray that I may know that His power is always available.

FEBRUARY 27   THOUGHT FOR THE DAY

When we came into this program, the first thing we did was to admit that we couldn't do anything about our affliction. We admitted that our problem was beyond our control. Until then, we could never decide whether or not to take precautions against it and always fell victim to it. And since we couldn't do anything about it ourselves, we put the whole problem in the hands of our Higher Power. Now we have nothing more to do with it, except to trust Him to take care of it for us. *Have I done this honestly and fully?*

MEDITATION FOR THE DAY

This is the time for my spirit to touch the spirit of God. I know that the feeling I experience in these moments is more important than all the sensations of material things. Just this moment's contact with God and with my thoughts, and all the fever of life leaves me. Then I am well, whole, and calm. Whatever the pressures, however often they return, this moment of spiritual sensing is all that I need to continue unperturbed another day.

PRAYER FOR THE DAY

I pray that the fevers of resentment, worry, fear, and envy may melt into nothing. I pray that health and serenity may take their place.

We should be free from our affliction for good. It is out of our hands when we turn it over to God. We don't need to worry about it or even think about it any more. But if we haven't done this honestly and fully, the chances are that it will return to torment us again. If we don't trust our Higher Power to take care of our problem, we reach out and take it back to ourselves. Then we're in the same situation we were in before, helpless once again and returned to madness. *Do I trust God to take care of the problem for me?*

MEDITATION FOR THE DAY

No work is of value without some preparation. Every work must have an adequate foundation on which to build. If we fail to provide one, what we try to build will eventually collapse. All the many hours of work will be profitless. In our effort we need spiritual preparation to achieve a sounder personal structure. Not the time in building but the quality of the effort is what attains results.

PRAYER FOR THE DAY

I pray that I may spend more time alone with God. I pray that then I may prepare for my life of new hope and freedom from turmoil.

FEBRUARY 29   THOUGHT FOR THE DAY

At times when I am concerned about whether or not I can continue to live the steps of this program, I think about past events. Most often I very quickly recall an event that still sends chills through me, and I wonder how it is that I'm able to sit here now. I might have been a hair away from total disaster, but somehow I got by. It wasn't skill or expertise or anything I did right. It was pure, stupid luck. I ask myself whether it is worth ever going back to that irrationality, and the answer is emphatically no. So I reread those steps and thank my Higher Power that I am alive to work them. *Do I remember my worst moments, to remind me how well off I am today?*

MEDITATION FOR THE DAY

As we wait for news of events that seem crucial to our lives, we sometimes reflect on what we might have done differently, were it all to be relived. This won't change the news we await, nor will it do much for history; but sometimes a little hindsight can be fruitful. The past tragic moments we've all shared were invariably devoid of a sense of the presence of a Higher Power. Had we that force at our side, things might have been different. While the past is now gone, the present can be filled with this new awareness, if we so wish. My Higher Power is big enough for everyone and needs only to be sought.

PRAYER FOR THE DAY

I pray that my pitiful failings are now no more than a memory. I pray that God will continue to bless me with inspiration, to show me what I might yet become.

MARCH 1 THOUGHT FOR THE DAY

When I find myself thinking about returning to that past irrational behavior, I remind myself, "Don't reach out and take that misery back." I gave that to God, and there's nothing I could do with it now but suffer. So I forget that kind of madness and put it out of my mind once more. I can do this because my Higher Power has given me enough control to avoid making that mistake. I've seen others try to do the same thing, lacking faith in a Higher Power to protect them. They invariably fail, as I often did in the past. *Have I determined never to take that problem back again?*

MEDITATION FOR THE DAY

Constant effort is necessary if I am to grow and to develop a spiritual life. I must keep the spiritual rules persistently, lovingly, patiently, and hopefully. By keeping them, every mountain of difficulty will be laid low, the rough places of poverty of spirit will be made smooth, and all who know me will know that my Higher Power is now Lord of all my ways. To get close to the spirit of God is to find life and healing and strength.

PRAYER FOR THE DAY

I pray that God's spirit may be everything I need. I pray that His spirit will help me discover life, healing, and strength.

Over a period of troubled years we've proved to ourselves and to everyone else that we can't stop our emotional excesses by will power. We have been totally helpless before them. So the only way we could stop was by turning to a Power greater than ourselves. Sometimes a person comes into this program only when everyone or everything else has failed. That Power remains as the only hope. So often it is the last-sought that is the only possible hope. Once we acknowledge His supremacy, we realize the sheer vanity of our delay. Surrender means that we put our life into God's hands. *Have I promised God that I will try to live the way He wants me to live?*

MEDITATION FOR THE DAY

The power of spiritual contact comes from communication with the Higher Power in prayer and times of quiet meditation such as this. I must constantly seek these moments, for they are my way to spiritual enlightenment. From this contact comes life, joy, peace, serenity. Others have their way, but for me this method works best.

PRAYER FOR THE DAY

I pray that I may feel that God's power is mine. I pray that I may be able to face anything that happens through that power.

MARCH 3   THOUGHT FOR THE DAY

After we have surrendered, the distressing problem is out of our hands and in the hands of our Higher Power. The thing we have to do is to be certain we never reach out and take the problem back again. Leave it in God's hands. Whenever I'm tempted to re-enter that past existence, I realize that it would not be the same, that I would do so knowing that I was contradicting what I've learned. *Is that knowledge enough to deter me? Do I have enough faith to turn aside from the urge?*

MEDITATION FOR THE DAY

My thoughts are not yet clear, although I have come a long way from that past state of calamity. I see some things distinctly, but others as though looking through an empty colored-glass bottle. I see warped images of the things beyond, and I have no true idea of their lightness or darkness. I know that one day, if I have faith and persist in the reasonable way, I will see things as they are, without distortion, in their true color.

PRAYER FOR THE DAY

I pray that God will show me new ways to assure that I will never return to my past turmoil. I pray that I may know how far I have already come with His guidance.

MARCH 4 THOUGHT FOR THE DAY

Even though we have given our problem to our Higher Power, we know that we will still be tempted at some time. We try to build up strength for that time when it comes. It helps a great deal to start the day right and to discipline our minds day after day to the rational life. We also avoid any associations and places that invariably led us into the disruptive pattern. These new habit patterns will help us retrain our attitudes, but we must also manage to re-educate our emotions to some degree by curbing the intensity of our reactions. *Am I now gradually taking things easy and changing my habit patterns?*

MEDITATION FOR THE DAY

The elimination of selfishness is one key to greater happiness, and can only be accomplished with faith. We must realize that we start with a spark of the Divine Spirit, but we have a large amount of innate selfishness. As we grow, and we come in contact with others, we can take either of two paths. We can become more selfish, extinguishing the Spirit, or we can develop spiritual awareness and strive for unselfishness.

PRAYER FOR THE DAY

I pray that I may grow more unselfish, honest, pure, and loving. I pray that I may take the right path every day

MARCH 5   THOUGHT FOR THE DAY

Sometimes we try too hard to get this program. It is better to relax, let it happen, for it will be given to us if we stop trying too hard. Emotional stability can be a free gift of God, which is given by His grace when He knows we are ready for it. That means that we will in time achieve self-control. But we have to be ready. We must know how to relax, to take it easy, and to accept the gift with gratitude and humility. The past troubles remain in the past, and my effort to overcome today's challenges is what occupies my time. *Do I realize that with God I will do today what I could never do by myself before?*

MEDITATION FOR THE DAY

Fear is the curse of the world. It is everywhere. I must fight fear as I would a plague. Fear is a useless emotion, and there is no room for it in the heart in which God dwells. Fear cannot exist where true love is or where faith abides. So I must have no fear. Fear destroys hope, and hope is necessary for all mankind.

PRAYER FOR THE DAY

I pray that I may have no fear. I pray that I may cast all fear out of my life.

MARCH 6 THOUGHT FOR THE DAY

Our first and imperative step on entering this program is to give up, admit that we're helpless against our affliction. We surrender our lives to a Higher Power and ask Him to help us, to take our burden. When He knows that we are ready, He gives us by His grace the free gift of sanity. We can't take credit for having conquered our irrationality, because we didn't have the power to do so by ourselves. There is no place in this program for pride or boasting. We can only be grateful to God for doing for us what we could never have done for ourselves. *Do I now believe that my Higher Power has made me a gift of the power to stay rational?*

MEDITATION FOR THE DAY

I must work with my Higher Power. One way is to do all I can to bring about a true fellowship of human beings. It helps me to help others, and I am slowly gaining a better contact with God, since this is how God works. I am more aware of His presence when I am doing His work. It is through the grace of God that any real change in human personality takes place. I therefore must rely on God's power, since anything I accomplish is through His help.

PRAYER FOR THE DAY

I pray that I may work for and with God. I pray that I may be used by Him to change human personalities for good.

There are two important things we have to do if we want to overcome our affliction and stay rational. First, having admitted that we are helpless before our affliction, we have to turn it over to a God of our understanding. This means asking Him every day for the strength to stay self-controlled that day and thanking Him every night. It means really leaving the problem in God's hands and not reaching out and taking it back. Second, when we have given our affliction to God, we must cooperate with Him by doing something about it ourselves. *Am I doing these two essential things?*

MEDITATION FOR THE DAY

I must prepare myself by doing each day what I can to develop physically, mentally, and spiritually. I can be sure that a test will come. Without proper training I cannot meet the test. I must want God's will for me above all else, and I must not expect to have what I am not prepared for. Meditation is a part of that preparation.

PRAYER FOR THE DAY

I pray that I may really try to do God's will in all my affairs. I pray that I may do all I can to help others find His will for them.

MARCH 8 THOUGHT FOR THE DAY

We must attend meetings regularly, if we are to learn to think differently. We must change our irrational thought processes to sane, rational ones and re-educate our minds. We must try to help others in turmoil. We must cooperate with our Higher Power by spending at least as much time and energy on this program as we did on our affliction. We must follow the program to the best of our ability and leave our problem in His hands. *Am I content to let God have my turmoil and to spend my effort on this program?*

MEDITATION FOR THE DAY

The joy of true fellowship will be mine in full measure, and I will revel in that joy. There will be returned as much as I am willing to share. Fellowship among spiritually-minded people is the embodiment of God's purpose for this world. To realize this will bring me a new joy of life. If I share in humanity's joy and travail, a greater understanding and blessing will be mine. I can truly live a life not of earth alone but of heaven also, here and now.

PRAYER FOR THE DAY

I pray that I may be helped and healed by true spiritual fellowship. I pray that I may sense God's presence in fellowship with His children.

If we had absolute faith in our Higher Power to keep us from all distress and if we turned our problems entirely over to Him without reservation, we would not have to do anything more about it. We'd be free from our afflictions once and for all. But since our faith is likely to be weak, we have to strengthen and build this faith. We do this in several ways. One way is by going to meetings and listening to others tell how they have found all the strength they need to overcome their turmoil. *Is my faith being strengthened by this personal witness of others afflicted?*

MEDITATION FOR THE DAY

It is the quality of my life that determines its value. In order to judge the value of a person's life, we must set up standards. The most valuable life is one of honesty, purity, unselfishness, and love. All people's lives ought to be judged by this standard in determining their value to the world. By this standard, most of the so-called heroes of history were not great men. "What shall it profit a man if he shall gain the whole world, and lose his own soul?"

PRAYER FOR THE DAY

I pray that I may be honest, pure, unselfish, and loving. I pray that I may make the quality of my life good by these standards.

We also strengthen our faith by working with others who have our affliction and finding that we can do nothing ourselves to help them except to tell them our own story of how we found the way out. If others are helped, it is by the grace of God and not by what we do or say. Our own faith is strengthened when we see others with our affliction find peace by turning to God. Finally, we strengthen our faith by having quiet moments each morning. *Do I ask my Higher Power in this quiet time for the strength to stay rational this day?*

MEDITATION FOR THE DAY

My five senses are my means of communication with the material world. They are the links between my physical life and the material manifestations around me. But I must sever all connections with the material world when I wish to hold communion with the Great Spirit of the universe. I have to hush my mind and bid all my senses be still before I can become attuned to receive the music of the heavenly spheres.

PRAYER FOR THE DAY

I pray that I may get my spirit in tune with the Spirit of the universe. I pray that through faith and communion with Him I may receive the strength I need.

By having our quiet moments each morning, we come to depend on the help of our Higher Power during the day, especially if we are tempted by our afflictions. And we can honestly thank Him each night for the strength He has given us. This daily meditation strengthens our faith, and there are other ways to do so. By listening to other members and working with them, we also strengthen our faith. *Have I tried through daily meditative moments to seek the help of the Higher Power and to thank Him?*

MEDITATION FOR THE DAY

It seems that sometimes when God wishes to express to us what He is like He creates a beautiful person. Think of a personality as God's expression of character attributes. Be as fit an expression of Godlike character as you can. When the beauty of a person's character is impressed upon us, it leaves an image that in turn reflects through our own actions. Look for beauty of character in those around you.

PRAYER FOR THE DAY

I pray that I may look at great persons until their beauty of character becomes a part of my soul. I pray that I may reflect this character in my own life.

The Prodigal Son took his journey into a far country and wasted his substance with riotous living. That is what those of us with afflictions do. The story continues that, when the son came to himself, he arose and went to his father. We do that, too, when we become a part of this program. That is when we come to our senses. The person steeped in distress is not the real self. The sane, sober, straight, rational, respectable person is the real self. Our involvement with our group has brought us happiness and a better self-image. *Have I come to see myself in a better light?*

MEDITATION FOR THE DAY

Simplicity is the keynote of a good life. Choose the simple things always. Life can become complicated if you let it become so. You can be swamped by difficulties if you let them take up too much of your time. Every difficulty can be either solved or ignored. Something better can be substituted for it. Love the humble things of life and revere the simple things. Your standard must never be the world's standard of wealth and power. These are ultimately sheer deception.

PRAYER FOR THE DAY

I pray that I may love the simple things of life. I pray that I may keep my life uncomplicated and free.

We've got rid of our false, overreacting selves and found our real, rational selves. And we turn to our Higher Power for help, just as the Prodigal Son arose and went to his father. At the end of that story the father said, "This my son was dead, and is alive again; he was lost and is found." All of us who are recovering through this program were certainly dead and are alive once more. We were lost and are found. *Am I grateful that I am alive again?*

MEDITATION FOR THE DAY

Gently breathe in God's spirit, that spirit which, if not barred out by selfishness, will enable you to do good works. This means that your Higher Power will be enabled to perform good works through you. You can become a channel for His spirit to flow through you and into the lives of others. The works that you can do will be limited only by your spiritual development. Let your spirit be in harmony with God's, and there will be no limits in human relationships.

PRAYER FOR THE DAY

I pray that I may become a channel of God's spirit. I pray that it may flow through me into the lives of those about me.

MARCH 14 THOUGHT FOR THE DAY

Can I get well? If I mean, "Can I ever tolerate my old turmoil again?" the answer is no. But if I mean, "Can I stay rational?" the answer is yes. I can get well by turning over to my Higher Power my emotional excesses, my proneness to frustration, and the turmoil that follows and by asking that Power each day to give me the strength to stay in control for the next twenty-four hours. I know from the experience of thousands of others that, if I honestly want to overcome distress, my Higher Power will help me do so. *Am I faithfully following this program?*

MEDITATION FOR THE DAY

Persevere in all that you are guided to do. The persistent carrying out of what seems right and good will bring you to that place where you would be. If you look back over God's guidance, you will see that His leading has been very gradual and that only as you have carried out His wishes, as far as you can understand them, has He been able to give you more clear and definite leading. You are led by God's touch on a quickened, responsive mind.

PRAYER FOR THE DAY

I pray that I may persevere in doing what seems right. I pray that I may carry out all of God's leading, to the best of my understanding.

As people in turmoil, we were on a merry-go-round and couldn't get off. It was a kind of hell on earth. In this program we got off that merry-go-round by learning how to retain control. I rely on my Higher Power, asking Him every morning to help me to keep control. And I get the strength from that Power to do what I could never do with my own strength alone. I do not doubt the existence of the God of my understanding. We do not speak into a vacuum when we pray. Our Higher Power is there. *Am I off the merry-go-round of turmoil for good?*

MEDITATION FOR THE DAY

I must remember that in spiritual matters I am only an instrument. It is not for me to decide how or when I am to act. God controls all spiritual matters. It is up to me to be fit to do God's work. All that hinders my spiritual activity must be eliminated. I can depend on Him for all the strength I need to overcome those faults that are obstacles. I must keep myself fit so that God can use me as a channel for His spirit.

PRAYER FOR THE DAY

I pray that selfishness may not hinder my progress in spiritual matters. I pray that I may be a good instrument for God to work with.

Before we decided to enter this program, most of us had to come up against a blank wall. We saw that we were beaten, that we had to have help. But we didn't know which way to turn for help. There seemed to be no doorway in that blank wall. This program opens the door that leads to recovery by encouraging us to admit honestly that we are powerless and to realize that we can't be irrational any longer. *Have I now gone through that doorway to control of my affliction?*

MEDITATION FOR THE DAY

I must have a singleness of purpose to do my part in God's work. I must not let material distractions interfere with my job of improving personal relationships. It is easy to become distracted by material affairs so that I lose my singleness of purpose. I do not have time to be concerned with the multifarious matters of the world, but must concentrate and specialize in what I can do best.

PRAYER FOR THE DAY

I pray that I may not become distracted by material affairs. I pray that I may concentrate on doing what I can do best.

This program also helps us to hold onto a rational life. By having regular meetings so that we can associate with others in the program who have experienced the same blank-wall dilemma, we are encouraged to tell the story of our own sad experiences with our affliction and thereby help others. Our attitude toward life changes from one of pride and selfishness to one of humility and gratitude. *Am I going to step back through that doorway in the wall to my past hopeless, ruinous, futile turmoil?*

MEDITATION FOR THE DAY

Withdraw into the calm of communion with God. Rest in that calm and peace, for when you are at home there, then it is that real life begins. Only when you are calm and serene can you do good work. Disturbances and upsets make you relatively useless. Calmness is based on complete trust in the Higher Power. Nothing in this world can separate you from the love of God.

PRAYER FOR THE DAY

I pray that I may wear the world like a loose garment. I pray that I may stay serene at the center of my world.

MARCH 18   THOUGHT FOR THE DAY

When we come into this program and face the fact that we must spend the rest of our lives without indulging in our excesses, it often seems too much for us. The program tells us to forget about the future and live just one day at a time. All we really have is now. We have no past time and no future time. Yesterday is gone; forget it. Tomorrow never comes; don't worry. Today is here; get busy. All we have is the present. *Am I living one day at a time?*

MEDITATION FOR THE DAY

Persistence is necessary if you are to advance to spiritual things. By prayer, persistence, and simple trust, you achieve the treasures of the spirit. By persistent practice you can eventually obtain joy, assurance, security, health, and serenity. Nothing is too great, in the spiritual realm, for you to obtain through persistent preparation for it.

PRAYER FOR THE DAY

I pray that I may persistently carry out my spiritual exercises every day. I pray that I may strive for peace and serenity.

MARCH 19   THOUGHT FOR THE DAY

When we were disoriented and confused, we were also ashamed of the past. Remorse is a terrible form of mental punishment. We felt ashamed of the things we had said and done. We were afraid to face people because of what they might think of us. We were afraid of the consequences of what we did when we were distraught. In this program we forget the past. I have done with the past. I have sought forgiveness for the past, no matter how black it was to me. *Now that I am honestly trying to do the right thing, can I forgive myself?*

MEDITATION FOR THE DAY

The spirit of the Higher Power is all about you all day long. You have no thoughts, plans, impulses, emotions that He does not know about. You could hide nothing from Him, even if you tried. Do not make your conduct conform only to the world, and do not depend on the approval or disapproval of others. God sees us in secret, but He rewards openly. If you are in harmony with the Divine Spirit, doing your best to live as God wants you to live, then you will be at peace.

PRAYER FOR THE DAY

I pray that I may always feel God's presence. I pray that I may realize His presence constantly all through the day.

MARCH 20 THOUGHT FOR THE DAY

When we were irrational, we used to worry about the future. Worry is another terrible form of mental anguish. We thought, "What's going to become of me? Where will I end up?" We could see ourselves slipping, getting gradually worse, and we wondered what the finish would be. Sometimes we got so discouraged worrying about the future that we thought of suicide. Our rationality was gone, and we were given over to insane fear at such times. *Have I stopped worrying about the future?*

MEDITATION FOR THE DAY

Functioning on the material plane alone will take me away from my Higher Power. Functioning on a spiritual plane as well as on a material one will make life what it should be. All material activities are valueless in themselves; but all activities, seemingly trivial or great, are alike if directed by God's guidance. I must try to obey God as I would expect a faithful, willing servant to carry out directions. Then on whatever plane I function, life will make sense.

PRAYER FOR THE DAY

I pray that the flow of God's spirit may come to me through many channels. I pray that I may function productively on all planes.

In this program we forget about the future. We know from experience that as time goes on the future takes care of itself. Everything works out well as long as we stay composed. All we need to concern ourselves with is today. We get up in the morning and see sunlight shining in the window. We thank God for another day to enjoy, because we are rational enough to appreciate it. This is a day in which we may have the chance to help somebody. *Do I know that this day is all that I have and that with God's help I can stay rational today?*

MEDITATION FOR THE DAY

All is well, fundamentally. That does not mean that all is well on the surface of things. It means that God has a purpose for the world that will eventually work out when enough of us are willing to follow His way. "Wearing the world as a loose garment" means not being upset by the surface wrongness of things but feeling deeply secure in the fundamental goodness and purpose in the universe.

PRAYER FOR THE DAY

I pray that God will be with me in my journey through this world. I pray that I may know that He is planning that journey.

We are all looking for the power to overcome our afflictions. We come into this program and ask, "How do I get the strength to recover?" At first it seems that there will never be the necessary strength. We see older members who have found the power we are looking for, but the process by which they found it is still a mystery. This necessary strength comes in many ways. *Have I found all the strength I need now?*

MEDITATION FOR THE DAY

You cannot have a spiritual need that God cannot supply. Your fundamental need is a spiritual one. It is the need for power to live the good life. The best spiritual supply is received by you when you want it to pass on to other people. You get it, then, by giving it away. That strength means increased health. This in turn means more good work, which in turn means more persons helped. And so it goes, a continuum to meet all spiritual needs.

PRAYER FOR THE DAY

I pray that my every spiritual need will be supplied by God. I pray that I may use the power I receive to help others.

Strength comes from the fellowship you find when you come into this program. Just being with men and women who have found the way out gives you a feeling of security. You listen to speakers, talk with other members, absorb the atmosphere of confidence and hope that you find there. You listen to situations that are not just like yours but that teach you a great deal. Seldom if ever do you come away without having received something of real value. *Am I receiving strength from this fellowship with others?*

MEDITATION FOR THE DAY

The Higher Power you have accepted is with you. Your faith must remain constant, and you must recognize that all power is His. Repeat it often, until you enjoy the safety and personal power it can mean to you. This knowledge drives back all threats and allows you to pass over temptations. You will begin to live a victorious life.

PRAYER FOR THE DAY

I pray that with strength from God I may lead an abundant life. I pray that I may lead a life of victory.

THOUGHT FOR THE DAY

Strength comes from honestly telling your own experiences with your affliction. In religion this is called confession. We call it witnessing or sharing. You give a personal witness, share your past, tell of the troubles you've had. For some there were hospitals, jails, a broken home, wasted money, debts, and countless foolish acts. This personal witness lets out the things you kept buried, brings them out into the open, and allows you to find both release and strength. *Am I receiving strength from my personal witnessing?*

MEDITATION FOR THE DAY

We cannot fully understand the universe. The simple fact is that we cannot even define space or time precisely. They are both boundless, in spite of all we can do to limit them. We live in a box of space and time we have manufactured by our own minds, and on that depends all our so-called knowledge of the universe. There is no way that we can ever know all things, nor are we made to know them. Much of our lives must be taken on faith.

PRAYER FOR THE DAY

I pray that my faith may be based on my own experience of the power of God in my life. I pray that I may know this one thing above all else in the universe.

Strength comes from belief in a Higher Power that can help you. You can't define this force, but you can see how it helps others like you who experience distress. You hear them talk about it, and you begin to get the idea yourself. You try praying in a quiet time each morning, and you begin to feel stronger, as though your prayers were answered. So you gradually come to accept that there must be a Power in the world outside yourself that is stronger than you and to which you can turn for help. *Am I receiving strength from my belief in a Higher Power?*

MEDITATION FOR THE DAY

Spiritual development is achieved by daily persistence in living the way you believe God wants you to live. Like the wearing away of ice by steady drops of water, so will your daily persistence wear away all difficulties and gain spiritual success for you. Never falter in this daily effort, but go forward boldly and unafraid. God will help you and strengthen you as long as you are trying to do His will.

PRAYER FOR THE DAY

I pray that I may persist day by day in gaining spiritual growth. I pray that I may make this a lifetime work.

Strength comes also from working with others who are distressed. When you are talking with prospects, you are building up your own strength at the same time. You see the others in the condition you might be in yourself, and it makes your resolve to stay rational stronger than ever. Often you help yourself more than the others, but if you do succeed in helping them to recover, you are stronger from the experience. *Am I receiving strength from working with others?*

MEDITATION FOR THE DAY

Faith is the bridge between us and our Higher Power. It is the bridge He has ordained. If all were seen and known, there would be no merit in doing right. Therefore, God has ordained that we do not see or know directly. But we can experience the power of His spirit through our faith. It is the bridge between God and us that we can cross or not cross, as we will. There could be no morality without free will. We must make the choice ourselves. We must make the venture of belief.

PRAYER FOR THE DAY

I pray that I may choose to cross the bridge of faith. I pray that by crossing that bridge I may receive the spiritual power I need.

You get the power to overcome your afflictions through the fellowship of others who have found the way out. You get power by honestly sharing your past experience through a personal witness. You get power by coming to believe in a Higher Power that can help you. Finally, you get power by working with others who suffer as you have. In these four ways thousands of distressed persons have found the power they needed to overcome their afflictions. *Am I ready and willing to accept this power and work for it?*

MEDITATION FOR THE DAY

The power of God's spirit is the greatest power in the universe. Our conquest of each other, the great kings and conquerors, the conquest of wealth, the leaders of the money society, all amount to very little in the end. Those who conquer themselves are greater than those who conquer cities. Material things have no permanence. But God's spirit is eternal. Everything really worthwhile in this world is the result of the power of His spirit.

PRAYER FOR THE DAY

I pray that I may open myself to the power of God's spirit. I pray that my relationships with my fellow beings may be improved by this spirit.

When you come to a meeting of this group, you are coming not just to a meeting but to a new life. I'm always impressed by the change I see in people after they've been in the group for a while. I sometimes take an inventory of myself, to see whether I have changed and, if so, in what way. Before I entered this program, I was very selfish. I wanted my own way in everything. I don't believe I ever grew up. When things went wrong, I sulked like a spoiled child and often let my emotions take over. *Am I now willing to give rather than receive?*

MEDITATION FOR THE DAY

There are two things that we must have if we are going to change our way of life. One is faith, the confidence in things unseen, in the fundamental goodness and purpose in the universe. The other is obedience, that is, living each day as we believe our Higher Power wants us to live, with gratitude, humility, honesty, unselfishness, and love. Faith and obedience will give us all the strength we need to live a new and more abundant life.

PRAYER FOR THE DAY

I pray that I may have more faith and obedience. I pray that I may live a more abundant life as a result of these things.

Before I entered this program, I was very dishonest. I lied to my closest friends, my mate, and others about where I had been and what I'd been doing. I took time off from work and pretended to be sick, or I gave some other dishonest excuse. I cheated myself as well as those I knew best. I would never face myself as I really was or admit when I was wrong. I pretended to myself that I was as good as anyone else, though I suspected I was not. *Am I now really aware of that past and determined to be honest?*

MEDITATION FOR THE DAY

I must live in the world and yet live apart with my Higher Power. I can go forth from my secluded times of communion with God and return to the work of the world. To get the spiritual strength I need, my inner life must be lived apart. I must wear the world as a loose garment. Nothing in the world should seriously upset me. All successful living arises from an inner life that is guided by the Higher Power.

PRAYER FOR THE DAY

I pray that I may live my inner life with God. I pray that nothing shall invade or destroy that secret place of peace.

MARCH 30   THOUGHT FOR THE DAY

Before I joined this group, I was very unloving. From the time I went to school, I paid very little attention to my parents. When I was on my own, I didn't even bother to keep in touch with them. After I got married, I was very unappreciative of my mate. Many times I left to have a good time. Later I paid too little attention to our children and didn't try to understand them or show them affection. My friends were really only companions, not real friends. *Have I got over loving no one but myself?*

MEDITATION FOR THE DAY

Be calm, be true, be quiet. Do not get overly excited about anything that happens around you. Feel a deep inner security in the goodness and purpose in the universe. Be true to your highest ideals. Do not slip back into the old ways of reacting. Stick to your spiritual guns. Do not talk back or defend yourself overmuch against accusation, whether false or true. Accept abuse just as you accept praise. Only God can judge you as you truly are.

PRAYER FOR THE DAY

I pray that I may not be upset by the judgment of others. I pray that I may let God be the judge of the real me.

MARCH 31   THOUGHT FOR THE DAY

Since I've been in this program, I have made a start toward being unselfish. I no longer want my own way in everything. When things go wrong and I can't have what I want, I no longer sulk. I am trying not to waste money on myself. And it makes me happy to see my mate with more money and also more for the children. It is very hard to resist the urge to think of myself first and foremost. How hard it is to lose that feeling, which was almost a religion before I turned my problems over to my Higher Power. *Am I trying to be unselfish?*

MEDITATION FOR THE DAY

Each day is a day of progress, if you make it so. You may not see it, but your Higher Power does. He does not judge by outward appearances. He judges by the heart. Let Him see in you a simple desire always to do His will. Though you may feel that your work has been spoiled or tarnished, God sees it as an offering for Him. When climbing a steep hill, you are often more conscious of the weakness of your stumbling feet than of the view, the grandeur, or even of the upward progress.

PRAYER FOR THE DAY

I pray that I may persevere in all good things. I pray that I may advance each day in spite of my stumbling feet.

APRIL 1   THOUGHT FOR THE DAY

Since I've entered this program, I've made a start toward becoming more honest. I no longer have to lie to my mate. I'm more often on time than late at work. I feel that I earn what I receive, and I can be hopeful again about future promotion. The hardest thing was facing myself as I really am, admitting along the way that I'm no good by myself. I have to rely on a Higher Power to help me become better and do the right things. I'm actually beginning to find what it means to be alive. *Am I facing the world honestly and without fear?*

MEDITATION FOR THE DAY

We had our lives all to ourselves, and it wasn't long before they were in shambles. We tried to get along without a Higher Power and made a grand mess of things. We could do nothing of any value to rectify matters, though we spent much time trying, until we finally realized that we needed something more. That something is the God of our understanding, and all our human relationships depend on this. When we let God's spirit rule our lives, we learn how to get along with others and how to help them. We learn to give and to receive, through His guidance.

PRAYER FOR THE DAY

I pray that I may let God run my life. I pray that I will never again make a shambles of my life through trying to run it myself.

APRIL 2 THOUGHT FOR THE DAY

Since I have been in this program, I have made a start toward becoming more loving to my family and friends. I visit my parents. I am more appreciative of my mate than I was before. I am grateful to them for having put up with me all those years. I have also found real companionship with my children. I've realized that the friends I've found in this program are real friends, who are always ready to help me, as I help them if I can. *Do I really care now about other people in my life?*

MEDITATION FOR THE DAY

Not what you do so much as what you are is the miracle-working power. You can be a force for good with the help of God. He is here to help you and to accompany you. Changed by His grace, you shed one garment of the spirit for a far better one. In time you put that one aside for a yet finer one. And so you are gradually transformed.

PRAYER FOR THE DAY

I pray that I may accept every challenge. I pray that each acceptance of a challenge may make me grow into a better man.

APRIL 3   THOUGHT FOR THE DAY

When I was distraught, I was absolutely selfish. I thought of myself first, last, and always. The universe revolved around me. When I awoke in the morning, my only thought was how terrible I felt. I wondered what I could do to make myself feel better. And the only thing I could think of was more distress. I couldn't see beyond myself and my need for this irrational turmoil. *Can I now look out and beyond my own selfishness?*

MEDITATION FOR THE DAY

Remember that the first quality of greatness is service. In a way, God is the greatest servant of all because He is always waiting for us to call on Him. His strength is always available to us, but we must ask it of Him through our own free will. It is a free gift, but we must sincerely seek it. A life of service is the finest life we can live. That is the beginning and the end of our real worth.

PRAYER FOR THE DAY

I pray that I may cooperate with God in all good things. I pray that I may serve Him and others and so lead a useful and happy life.

APRIL 4　THOUGHT FOR THE DAY

When I came into this program, I found men and women who had been through the same things I had experienced. But now they were thinking more about how they could help others than they were about themselves. They were a lot more unselfish than I ever was. By coming to meetings and associating with them, I began to think a little less about myself and a little more about others. I learned that I didn't have to depend on myself but could get greater strength than my own. *Am I now depending less on myself and more on God?*

MEDITATION FOR THE DAY

You cannot help others unless you understand the persons you are trying to help. To understand the problems and trials of others, you must do all you can to understand others. You must study their backgrounds, their likes and dislikes, their reactions and prejudices. When you see their weaknesses, do not confront them with them. Share *your* weaknesses, *your* failures, *your* temptations, and let others form their own convictions.

PRAYER FOR THE DAY

I pray that I may serve as a vehicle for God's power to come into the lives of others. I pray that I may try to understand them better.

APRIL 5   THOUGHT FOR THE DAY

People often ask what makes this program work. One of the answers is that it works because it gets a person away from himself as the center of things. It teaches him to rely more on the fellowship of others and on the strength of a Higher Power. Forgetting ourselves in fellowship, prayer, and working with others is what makes the program work. *Are these things keeping me rational?*

MEDITATION FOR THE DAY

God is the great interpreter of one human personality to another. Even those who are the closest have much in their natures that remain a sealed book to each other. Only as God enters and controls their lives are the mysteries of each revealed to the other. Each personality is so different that God alone understands the language of each and can interpret between them. Here we find the miracle of change and the true interpretation of life.

PRAYER FOR THE DAY

I pray that I may be in the right relationship to God. I pray that He will interpret to me the personalities of others, that I may understand them and help them.

All the people in this program had a personality problem. They used their emotions or some crutch to escape from life, to counteract feelings of loneliness or inferiority, or because of some conflict within. They could not adjust to life. This is a symptom of the affliction. They could not stop drinking, using drugs, eating, gambling, being abusive until they found a way to solve their personality problem. That's why going through forced denial solves nothing. Taking some sort of pledge doesn't work, either. *Was my problem ever solved by making these futile efforts?*

MEDITATION FOR THE DAY

God irradiates your life with the warmth of His spirit. You must open up like a flower to this divine force, loosen your hold on earth, its cares, its worries. Unclasp your hold on material things, relax your grasp, and the tide of peace and serenity will flow in. Relinquish every material thing you cherish, and then receive it back again from God. Do not hold onto earth's treasures so firmly that your hands are too full to clasp God's hand, as He extends it to you in love.

PRAYER FOR THE DAY

I pray that I may be open to receive God's blessing. I pray that I may be willing to relinquish my hold on material things and receive them back from God.

APRIL 7   THOUGHT FOR THE DAY

In this program sufferers find a way to solve personality problems. They do this by recovering three things. First, they recover their personal integrity. They pull themselves together. They get honest with themselves and with other people. They face themselves and their problems honestly instead of running away. They take personal inventories to see where they really stand. Then they face the facts instead of making excuses. *Have I recovered my integrity?*

MEDITATION FOR THE DAY

When trouble comes, do not say, "Why should this happen to me?" Leave yourself out of the picture. Think of others and their troubles. Then you will forget about your own. Gradually get away from yourself, and you will know the consolation of unselfish service to others. After a while it will not matter so much what happens to you. It is not so important anymore, except as your experience can be used to help others who are in the same kind of trouble.

PRAYER FOR THE DAY

I pray that I may become more unselfish. I pray that I may not be slowed in my progress by letting the old selfishness creep back into my life.

Second, distressed people recover their faith in a Power greater than themselves. They admit that they are helpless by themselves, and they call on that Higher Power for help. They surrender their lives to God as they understand him. They put their emotions, their problems in God's hands and leave them there. They recover their faith in a Higher Power that can help. *Have I recovered my faith?*

MEDITATION FOR THE DAY

You must make a stand for God. Believers in God are considered by some to be peculiar people. You must be willing to be deemed a fool for the sake of your faith. You must be ready to stand aside and let the fashions and customs of the world go by, when God's purposes are thereby forwarded. Be known by the marks that distinguish a believer in God. These are honesty, purity, unselfishness, love, gratitude, and humility.

PRAYER FOR THE DAY

I pray that I may be ready to profess my belief in God before others. I pray that I may not be turned aside by the skepticism or cynicism of nonbelievers.

Third, distraught people recover their proper relationship with others. They think less about themselves and more about others. They try to help others who suffer the same turmoil. They make new friends so they are no longer lonely. They try to live a life of service rather than selfishness, and all relationships with others are thereby improved. They solve their personality problems by recovering personal integrity, their faith in a Higher Power, and their way of fellowship and service to others. *Am I recovering my relationship with others?*

MEDITATION FOR THE DAY

All things that depress you, all that you fear, are really powerless to harm you. These things are but phantoms. So arise from earth's bonds, from depression, distrust, fear, and all that hinder your new life. Arise to beauty, joy, peace, and work inspired by love. Arise from death to life anew, for you do not need to fear even death. All past transgressions are forgiven if you live and love and work with God. Let nothing hinder your new life. Seek to know more and more of the new way of living.

PRAYER FOR THE DAY

I pray that I may let God live in me as I work for Him. I pray that I may go out into the sunlight and work with God.

APRIL 10   THOUGHT FOR THE DAY

When I came into this program, I came into a new world, a saner, sensible world of rationality, peace, serenity, and happiness. But I know that if I relapse just one time I'll go right back into that old world. That world of turmoil, that insane world of conflict and misery, is not a pleasant place for me. Looking at the world from the bottom of a void is terrifying. *Do I want to go back into that chaotic, irrational world?*

MEDITATION FOR THE DAY

Pride stands sentinel at the door of the heart and shuts out the love of God. God can dwell only with the humble and the obedient. Obedience to His will is the key unlocking the door to God's kingdom. You cannot obey God to the best of your ability without realizing His love and responding to it. The rough stone steps of obedience lead up to where the mosaic floor of love and joy is laid. Where God's spirit is, there is your home. There is heaven for you.

PRAYER FOR THE DAY

I pray that God may make His home in my humble and obedient heart. I pray that I may obey His guidance to the best of my ability.

In that distressing world of the past one excess always leads to another, and you can't stop till you're totally involved again. And the next day it begins all over again, until you eventually end up in jail, in a hospital, broke. You lose your job, your home, your family. You're on the merry-go-round again, and you can't get off. The fence is too high, and you can't get out. *Am I convinced that such turmoil is no place for me?*

MEDITATION FOR THE DAY

I must learn to accept self-discipline. I must try never to yield a single point that I have won. I must not let myself go and indulge in resentments, hates, fears, pride, lust, or gossip. If this discipline separates me from some people who are without discipline, I will carry on with different ways and a different standard of living. I may be actuated by motives that are different from others, but I will try to live the way I believe God wants me to live, no matter what others say.

PRAYER FOR THE DAY

I pray that I may be an example to others of a better way of living. I pray that I may carry on in spite of hindrances.

APRIL 12   THOUGHT FOR THE DAY

This sober, sane, rational world is a pleasant place for people like you and me to live in, once we've escaped the chaotic daze. We find real friends in the group. We again feel good in the morning. We find jobs, find ways to get things done in many areas. Our families and intimate friends welcome us because once more we are human and feeling. So many subtle yet good things begin to happen once more, after years of misery, torment, and distress. *Am I convinced that this rediscovered world is the right place for me to live in?*

MEDITATION FOR THE DAY

Our need is God's opportunity. First, we must recognize our need. Often this means helplessness before some weakness or sickness and an admission of our need for help. Next comes faith in the power of God's spirit, available to us to meet that need. Before any need can be met, our faith must find expression. That expression of faith is all God needs to manifest His power in our lives. Faith is the key that unlocks the storehouse of God's resources.

PRAYER FOR THE DAY

I pray that I may first admit my needs. I pray that then I may have faith that God will meet those needs in the way that is best for me.

Now that I've found my way into this new world by the grace of God and the help of this program, I am not going to take that step backward. Just one step backward will change my whole world again. I will not deliberately go back to the suffering of that irrational world. I'll hold onto the happiness of this new world, now that I've experienced the difference. *With God's help, am I going to hold onto this program with both hands?*

MEDITATION FOR THE DAY

I will try to help make the world better and happier by my presence in it. I will try to help other people find the way God wants them to live. I will try to be on the side of good, in the stream of righteousness, where all things work for good. I will do my duty persistently and faithfully, not sparing myself. I will be gentle with all people. I will try to see other people's difficulties and help them to resolve them. I will always pray that God will act as interpreter between me and others.

PRAYER FOR THE DAY

I pray that I may live in the spirit of prayer. I pray that I may depend on God for the strength I need to help me to do my part in making the world a better place.

APRIL 14   THOUGHT FOR THE DAY

Hospital personnel tell of cases they have encoun-
tered over the years, the causes of tragedy being turmoil and uncontrolled emotions. One young man
was burned by gasoline thrown on him and ignited
by his outraged wife, while he lay on the bed, drunk.
A woman lived in fear of her life, after being attacked
by a desperate man. Another man lost his sanity from
using drugs recklessly. *When I read or hear such stories,
do I count the ways I can gratefully say, "But for the grace
of God"?*

MEDITATION FOR THE DAY

I must maintain balance by keeping spiritual things at
the center of my life. God will give me this poise and
balance if I pray for it. This poise will give me power
in dealing with others. This balance will manifest itself more and more in my own life. I will keep material things in their proper place and keep spiritual
things at the center of my life. Then I will be at peace
amid the distractions of everyday living.

PRAYER FOR THE DAY

I pray that I may dwell with God at the center of my
life. I pray that I may keep that inner peace at the
center of my being.

APRIL 15   THOUGHT FOR THE DAY

Terrible things could have happened to any one of us. We never will know what might have happened to us when we were thrown into turmoil. We usually thought, "That couldn't happen to me!" But any one of us could have easily caused loss of life or lost our own lives if we had become distraught enough. But fear of these things never kept any of us from becoming irrational. That is the dangerous nature of our affliction. *Do I believe that in this program we have something more effective than fear?*

MEDITATION FOR THE DAY

I must keep calm and unmoved by the vicissitudes of life. I must go back into the silence of communion with my Higher Power to recover this calm when I lose it even for a moment. I will accomplish more by this calmness than by all the activities of a long day. At all cost I will keep calm. I can solve nothing when I am agitated. I should keep away from things that are emotionally upsetting. I must run on an even keel and not get tipped over by trying events. I should seek for things that are serene, good, and rewarding and stay with them.

PRAYER FOR THE DAY

I pray that I may not argue or contend but merely state calmly what I believe to be true. I pray that I may stay calm through faith.

APRIL 16   THOUGHT FOR THE DAY

In this program we have a kind of insurance, which is our faith in a Higher Power. It protects us against the terrible things that might happen to us if we ever become deeply distressed again. By putting our problem in the hands of God, we've taken out a policy that insures us against the ravages of our kind of insanity, as our homes are insured against the ravages of fire. *Am I paying my program insurance premiums regularly?*

MEDITATION FOR THE DAY

I must try to love my fellow man. Love comes from thinking of every man or woman as my brother or sister, because we are all children of God. This way of thinking makes me care enough about them to really want to help them. I must put this kind of love into action by serving others. Love means no severe judging, no resentments, no malicious gossip, and no destructive criticism. It also means patience, understanding, compassion, and helpfulness.

PRAYER FOR THE DAY

I pray that I may realize that God loves me, since He is the Father of us all. I pray that I, in turn, may have love for all of His children.

Every time we go to a group meeting, every time we say the Lord's Prayer, every time we have a quiet time before breakfast, we're paying a premium on our insurance against the recurrence of the old turmoil. And every time we help another member, we're making a large payment on our rationality insurance. We're making sure that our policy does not lapse. *Am I building up an endowment in serenity, peace, and happiness that will assure me of adequate coverage the rest of my life?*

MEDITATION FOR THE DAY

I gain faith by my own experience of God's power in my life. The constant, persistent recognition of His spirit in all my personal relationships is evident. The ever-accumulating evidence of His guidance is indisputable, the numberless instances in which seeming chance or wonderful coincidence can be traced to His purpose in my life are uncanny. All these things gradually engender a feeling of wonder, humility, and gratitude to God. These in turn are followed by a more sure and abiding faith in God and His purposes.

PRAYER FOR THE DAY

I pray that my faith may be strengthened every day. I pray that I may find confirmation of my life in the good things that have come into my life.

As I look back over my turmoil and affliction, have I learned that you take out of life what you put into it? When I put trouble and chaos into my life, I took out a lot of misery and bad things. Hospitals with all manner of problems, convulsions, overdose, suicide attempts, psychiatric tests; jail; loss of job; broken home; divorce and custody conflicts. When I put madness like that into my life, is it any wonder I got madness out? *Do I remember now that I must be careful what I put into my life?*

MEDITATION FOR THE DAY

I should strive for a friendliness and helpfulness that will affect all who come near to me. I should try to see something to love in them all. I should welcome them, bestow little courtesies and understanding on them, and help them if they ask for it. I must send no one away without a word of cheer, a feeling that I really care about him. God may have put the impulse in some despairing one's mind to come to me. I must not fail Him by repulsing that person.

PRAYER FOR THE DAY

I pray that I may warmly welcome all who come to me for help. I pray that I may make them feel that I truly care.

Since I've been putting more sanity into my life, I've been taking out a lot of better things. I can describe it best as a kind of quiet satisfaction. I feel good. I feel right with the world, on the right side of the fence. As long as I put rationality into my life, almost everything I take out is good. The satisfaction I get out of living a saner life is made up of a lot of little things. I have the ambition to do things I didn't feel like doing when I was so distressed. *Am I getting satisfaction out of living a sensible life?*

MEDITATION FOR THE DAY

It is a glorious way, the upward-moving way. There are wonderful discoveries in the realm of the spirit. There are tender intimacies in the quiet times of communion with the God of your understanding. There is an amazing, almost incomprehensible understanding of others. On the upward way, you can have all the strength you need from your Higher Power. He is inexhaustible, giving you all the power you need as long as you move the upward way.

PRAYER FOR THE DAY

I pray that I may see the beautiful horizons ahead on the upward way. I pray that I may keep moving forward to a more abundant life.

The satisfaction you get out of living a rational life is made up of a lot of little things, but they add up to a satisfactory and happy life. You take out of life what you put into it. So you say to people coming into this program: "Don't worry about what life will be like without the turmoil you have had. Just stay with it, and a lot of good things will happen for you. And you'll have that feeling of quiet satisfaction and peace, of serenity and gratitude." *Is my life becoming really satisfying?*

MEDITATION FOR THE DAY

There are two paths we may take, one up and one down. We have been given free will to choose either path. We are captains of our souls to this extent only. We can choose the good or the bad. If we choose the wrong path, we go down, eventually to death. But if we choose the right path, we go up and up, until we come to eternal happiness. On the wrong path, we have no power for good because we do not choose to ask for it. But on the right path, we are on the side of good. We have all the power of God's spirit with us.

PRAYER FOR THE DAY

I pray that I may be in the stream of goodness. I pray that I may be on the right side, on the side of all good in the universe.

After we've been in this program for a while, we find out that if we're going to remain rational we have to be humble people. All the others we see in our group who have really succeeded are humble people. When I stop to think that but for the grace of God I might be deranged right now, I can't help feeling humble. Gratitude to God for His grace makes me humble. When I think of the kind of person I was not too long ago, when I think of the person I left behind me, I am humbly grateful that that life is over. *Am I grateful and humble?*

MEDITATION FOR THE DAY

I must arise from the death of deceit and selfishness and put on a new life of integrity. All the old ways and old temptations must be laid in the grave and a new existence made to rise from the ashes. Yesterday is gone, and all my errors are forgiven. I am honestly trying to do God's will today. Today is here, and it is the time of my resurrection and renewal. I must start now to build a new life of complete faith and trust in my Higher Power and a determination to do His will in all things.

PRAYER FOR THE DAY

I pray that I may share in making the world a better place to live. I pray that I may do what I can to bring goodness a little nearer to this earth.

People believe in this program when they see it work. An actual demonstration is what convinces them. What they read in books or hear people say doesn't convince them. But when they see a real honest-to-goodness change take place in another person, a change from an irrational being to a sane, useful citizen, that is something they can believe. There is one thing that proves to me that this program works. *Have I seen changes in others who came into my group?*

MEDITATION FOR THE DAY

There are conditions necessary for a spiritual life. One must accept obedience to a Higher Power and be willing to submit to His control. It takes time to develop this faith and trust and to believe that He is the Divine Principle in the universe. Unquestioning obedience is difficult. It means living each day the way you believe God wants you to live. Having overcome grievous turmoil and by frequently seeking His guidance, you can gradually develop a new way of life, doing the right thing at all times.

PRAYER FOR THE DAY

I pray that I will serve God, practicing unhesitating obedience. I pray that, as I gradually improve, I may find a new way of life that makes me useful.

Men and women come into this program defeated by their affliction, often given up by doctors and others as hopeless. They admit that they are helpless to conquer their affliction. When I see these people acquire serenity and stay rational over a period of months and years, I know that this program works. The changes I see in people who come into the program not only convince me that it works but also convince me that there must be a Power greater than ourselves that helps us change. *Am I convinced that a Higher Power can help me to change and remain so?*

MEDITATION FOR THE DAY

Cooperation with God is the great necessity for our lives. All else follows naturally. Cooperation with Him is the result of our consciousness of His presence. Guidance is bound to come to us as we live more and more with God, and as our consciousness becomes more attuned to the way of the universe. We must have many quiet times when we acknowledge our need to be led and feel His presence. New spiritual growth comes naturally from cooperation with God.

PRAYER FOR THE DAY

I pray that God may supply me with strength and show me the direction in which He wants me to grow. I pray that these things may come naturally from my cooperation with Him.

It has been proved that we afflicted persons cannot recover by our own will power. We've failed again and again. Therefore, I believe that there must be a Higher Power that helps us. I think of that Power as the grace of God. And I pray every morning for the strength to stay rational today. I know that Power is there because it never fails to help me. *Do I believe that this program works through the grace of God to help me?*

MEDITATION FOR THE DAY

Once I am "born of the spirit," that is my life's breath. Within me is the Life of life, so that I can never perish. The Life down through the ages has kept God's children through peril, adversity, and sorrow. I must try never to doubt or worry but to follow where the Life leads me. How often, when I am least aware, God goes before me to prepare the way, soften a heart, or put aside a resentment. As the Life spirit grows, my natural wants become less important.

PRAYER FOR THE DAY

I pray that my life may become centered in God more than in myself. I pray that my will may be directed toward doing His will.

I believe that this program works not because I read it in a book or heard people say so but because I see people becoming rational and staying that way. An actual demonstration is what convinces me. When I see that change in people, I can't help believing that the program works. We can listen to people talk in our group all day, and not believe it. But when we see the change in them, we have no choice but to believe. *Do I see this program work every day?*

MEDITATION FOR THE DAY

All of us find it extremely hard to be friendly or to give our support and approval to someone we do not like. We find it just as hard to be benevolent toward a person we know is in trouble through choice or intent. In the end it is easier and more honest to let our Higher Power do the blessing and the correcting. We must learn to reserve our worship to God and to leave His work to Him. We must occupy ourselves with ourselves and what He would have us do. If we do this, we will find that He guides us to attain the other things as well.

PRAYER FOR THE DAY

I pray that I may accept God's blessing so that I will be able to deal with those whom I find it hard to accept. I pray that I may do what He would have me do.

This program is one of submission, release, and action. When we were irrational, we were submitting to a power greater than ourselves—our affliction. Our self-wills were no use against the power. One encounter and we were completely adrift. In our group we stop submitting to the power of our affliction. Instead we submit to a Higher Power, greater than ourselves. *Have I submitted myself to that Higher Power?*

MEDITATION FOR THE DAY

Ceaseless activity is not God's plan for your life. Times of withdrawal for renewal of strength are always necessary. When you feel the faintest tremor of fear, stop all work. Stop everything and rest until you are strong again. Deal in the same manner with tiredness, for then you need rest of body. You cannot expect to do all things, depending upon the Higher Power to keep you from exhaustion. His supply of power is intended for things you believe He wants you to do. Physical and mental fatigue are yours to control.

PRAYER FOR THE DAY

I pray that I may learn how to rest and to listen, as well as how to work. I pray that I may know when to withdraw for renewal of strength.

By submitting to a Higher Power, we are released from the power of our affliction. It has no more hold on us. We are also released from the things that were holding us down, such as pride, selfishness, and fear. And we are free to grow into a new life, which is so much better than the old life. This release gives us serenity and peace with the world. *Have I been released from the power of my affliction?*

MEDITATION FOR THE DAY

We know our Higher Power by spiritual vision. We feel that He is beside us. Such contact is made not by the senses but through a spiritual consciousness that replaces other senses. Many people have been able to attain this state of spiritual consciousness, and yet none truly understand it or can explain it. This is the power of faith, which we find so vital in our endeavor to reconcile our lives to this new direction.

PRAYER FOR THE DAY

I pray that I may have a consciousness of God's presence. I pray that He will give me spiritual vision.

APRIL 28   THOUGHT FOR THE DAY

We're so glad to be free from turmoil that we do something about it. We get into action. We come to meetings regularly. We try to help others in distress. We pass on the good news whenever we have the chance. In a spirit of thankfulness to our Higher Power we get into action. This program is simple. Submit yourself to a God of your understanding, find release from your deep distress, and get into action. Do these things and keep doing them, and you will be well prepared for the rest of your life. *Since I came into this program, have I succeeded in getting into action?*

MEDITATION FOR THE DAY

Where does one look for those who are lost? The places are endless, even among crowds. We find a great satisfaction in following where our Leader would have us go, where we can lend our helping hand. We are bringing good news into places where it has not been known before. Sometimes we cannot tell which ears hear us, but we can leave all results to God. Many will hear us, just as we heard.

PRAYER FOR THE DAY

I pray that I may follow God in His eternal quest for souls. I pray that I may offer my helping hand.

Our program is one of faith, hope, and charity. It is a program of hope because, when new members come into it, the first thing they gain is new hope. They hear the older members tell how they have been through the same kind of hell and how they found the way out through this program. And this gives them hope that if others could do it they also can do it. Hope does not instantly flower, but it grows with persistence. *Is hope strong in me and growing steadily?*

MEDITATION FOR THE DAY

The rule of God's kingdom is perfect order, perfect harmony, perfect supply, perfect love, perfect honesty, perfect obedience. There is no discord in God's kingdom, but only things still unconquered in us. Most of our difficulties are caused by disharmony of one sort or another. We lack power because we lack harmony with a Higher Power and with each other. It may seem that He fails if that power is not manifested in our lives. God does not fail. People fail because they are out of harmony with Him.

PRAYER FOR THE DAY

I pray that I may be in harmony with God and with others. I pray that this harmony will result in strength and success.

APRIL 30   THOUGHT FOR THE DAY

Our program is one of faith because we find that we must have faith in a Power greater than ourselves if we are to become rational. We're helpless before these afflictions, but when we turn our distress over to God, develop faith that He provides strength, then our turmoil is stilled at last. Faith in that Divine Principle in the universe is essential in our program. It is something one cannot know without reaching out for it. *Is my faith strong in me?*

MEDITATION FOR THE DAY

Every person is a child of God and as such is full of promise of spiritual growth. A young person is like the springtime of the year. The full time of the fruit is not yet, but there is promise in the blossom. Each of us has some of God's spirit, which we develop by spiritual exercise. We continually need this exercise, just as the plant continually needs soil, water, sunlight. Our lives have been touched by a blight, which need not destroy the blossoming or prevent fruition later. Our growing cycle, with His help, continues.

PRAYER FOR THE DAY

I pray that I may develop all that is within my capacity to flower and bear fruit. I pray that I may receive His promise of a more abundant life.

MAY 1   THOUGHT FOR THE DAY

This program is one of charity, because the real meaning of charity is caring enough about others to want to help them. To get the full benefit of the program, we must try to help other members. We may try to help somebody and think we have failed, but the seed we have planted may bear fruit at some later time. We never know the results that even a word of ours might have. But the main thing is to have charity for others, a real desire to help them, whether or not we succeed. *Do I have a feeling of genuine charity?*

MEDITATION FOR THE DAY

All material things, the universe, the world, even our bodies, may be Eternal Thought expressed in time and space. The more physicists and astronomers reduce matter, the more it becomes a mathematical expression, which is thought. In the final analysis, is matter thought? When Eternal Thought expresses itself within the framework of time and space, it is hypothesized as matter. Our thoughts are finite, and we know only material things. But we deduce that outside the space-time limit is Eternal Thought, which we can call the God of our understanding.

PRAYER FOR THE DAY

I pray that I may be a true expression of Eternal Thought. I pray that God's thought may work through me.

MAY 2   THOUGHT FOR THE DAY

In our group we often hear the slogan "Easy Does It."
We who suffer our affliction always do everything to
excess. We indulge our emotions. We worry too
much. We have too many resentments. We tend to be
addictive. We tend to hurt ourselves physically, mentally, and spiritually by too much of everything.
When we come into this program, we have to learn to
take it easy. None of us knows how much longer we
have to live. It's probable that some of us wouldn't
have lived much longer if we had continued the way
we were going. By stopping that kind of insanity, we
have increased our chances of living for a good while
longer. *In the time I've been a member, have I learned to
practice "Easy Does It"?*

MEDITATION FOR THE DAY

You must be, before you can do. To accomplish
much, be much. The doing must be the expression of
the being. It is foolish to believe that we can accomplish much in personal relationships without first
preparing ourselves by being honest, pure, unselfish,
and loving. We will be given opportunities when we
are able and worthy. Our quiet moments are good
preparation for creative action.

PRAYER FOR THE DAY

I pray that I may constantly prepare myself for better
things to come. I pray that I may have opportunities
when I am ready for them.

MAY 3   THOUGHT FOR THE DAY

This program teaches us to take it easy. We learn how to relax and to stop worrying about the past or the future. We learn to give up our resentments, hates, and tempers. We try to stop being critical of others and to try to help them instead. That's why "Easy Does It" is important to us. In the time that is left to me, I'm going to try to take it easy, to relax, to avoid worry, and to be helpful to others. *For what is left of my life, is my motto going to be "Easy Does It"?*

MEDITATION FOR THE DAY

I must overcome myself before I can truly forgive other people for injuries done to me. The self in me cannot forgive injuries. The very thought of wrongs means that my self is in the foreground. Since the self cannot forgive, I must overcome my selfishness. I must cease trying to concern myself with those who disturbed and wronged me. It is a mistake for me even to think about those events. I must overcome myself in daily living, and then I will find that there is nothing in me that needs to remember injury. Only my selfishness was injured, and that is gone.

PRAYER FOR THE DAY

I pray that I may hold no resentments. I pray that my mind may be washed clean of all past hates and fears.

When I was in deep turmoil, I always tried to build myself up. I told myself tall stories about my own capacities. I told them so often that I half-believed some of them. I used to criticize others so that I could feel superior to them. The reason I always tried to build myself up was that I thought I really didn't amount to much. It was a kind of defense against my feeling of inferiority. *Do I still need to build myself up?*

MEDITATION FOR THE DAY

God thought about the universe and brought it into being. Such a thing is beyond our capacity to comprehend. But we can think, on our human level. During our hours of turmoil we were intellectually barren, or we would have thought of ways to end the suffering. It requires years to train one's mind. It is the work of a lifetime to develop to full spiritual stature. A fine mind that lacks the spirit is useless. Having both is what gives real meaning to life.

PRAYER FOR THE DAY

I pray that I may have God's thoughts as I live my life. I pray that I may live as He wants me to live.

MAY 5 THOUGHT FOR THE DAY

I had to show off and boast, sometimes out of embarrassment and awkwardness, so that others would think that I was calm, collected, capable, and sharp. Both they and I knew that this wasn't true. I didn't fool anyone. Since then I've become more rational, but that old habit of building myself up is still with me. I still have a tendency to show off and to pretend to be more than I am. *Am I on guard against conceit now that I'm becoming rational?*

MEDITATION FOR THE DAY

I cannot ascertain the spiritual realm with my intellect. I can only do so by my faith and spiritual faculties. My intellect perceives the results, but I must think of God with my heart rather than with my head. I can virtually breathe in His spirit in the life about me. I can keep my eyes focused on the good things in the world. I am enclosed in a box of time and space, but I have a window in my faith. If I want, I can empty my mind of all limitations of material things. I can sense the Eternal.

PRAYER FOR THE DAY

I pray that whatever is good I may have. I pray that I may leave to God the choice of what good will come to me.

MAY 6   THOUGHT FOR THE DAY

I have noticed that those who do the most for this program are not in the habit of boasting about it. The real danger of building myself up is that I may have a fall. That pattern goes with my affliction. If one side of the boat gets too high, the other gets dangerously low, and the boat is likely to tip over. Building a false ego is not the same as recovery. If I am to stay rational, I have to avoid radical ways, a false ego, and any other easy way out. *Have I got the right perspective of what it takes to stay rational?*

MEDITATION FOR THE DAY

The way of recovery sometimes seems long and weary. So many people today are weary. When the weary and the heavy-laden share their need to find rest by coming to me, I should help them find what I have found. The cure for world-weariness is to turn to spiritual things. That implies daring to suffer, to conquer selfishness, and to find spiritual peace in the face of all the weariness of the world.

PRAYER FOR THE DAY

I pray that I may be a help to discouraged people. I pray that I may help show others how to find what the weary world needs.

MAY 7   THOUGHT FOR THE DAY

It is very important to keep a grateful frame of mind, if we want to stay rational. We should be grateful that we're living in a day and age when distressed persons aren't treated as they often used to be, before this program was started. In the old days, each town had its drunk, its retarded person, its obsessed one. They were regarded with scorn and ridiculed by the townspeople. When we came into this program, we found all the sympathy, understanding, and fellowship that we could ask for. *Am I grateful to be a member?*

MEDITATION FOR THE DAY

Spiritual success is a joint effort between man and God. We must put forth effort. We cannot lean on our oars and drift with the tide. We must often direct our efforts against the tide of materialism around us. When difficulties come, our efforts are needed to surmount them. God directs our effort into the right channel, and His power helps us choose the right way.

PRAYER FOR THE DAY

I pray that I may choose the right way. I pray that I may have God's blessing and direction in all my efforts for good.

MAY 8   THOUGHT FOR THE DAY

I'm grateful that I found a program that could keep me rational. I'm thankful it has shown me the way to have faith in a Higher Power, because the renewing of that faith has changed my way of life. I have found a happiness and contentment that I had forgotten existed. By accepting a God of my understanding and living the kind of life that I know He wants me to live, I am following what this program offers. As long as I stay grateful, I'll remain rational. *Am I in a grateful frame of mind today?*

MEDITATION FOR THE DAY

As I recover more each passing day, I learn things about me that I did not know before. I learn to go very slowly, very quietly from one duty to the next, taking time to rest between. I learn not to be too busy, learn to take everything in order. Rest and meditation with my Higher Power afford peace and invariably lead to better work. I can claim the power from God to help work miracles in human lives. I see these lives change before my eyes. Prayer and rest are imperative. They are also crucial to understanding others.

PRAYER FOR THE DAY

I pray that I may not be in too much of a hurry. I pray that I may take time out often to rest with God.

MAY 9 THOUGHT FOR THE DAY

We used so little self-control when we were in turmoil. We were absolutely selfish, and so now it does us good to give up something once in a while. Using self-discipline and denying ourselves a few things are good for us, provided we don't go to extremes. At first, giving up irrational conduct is a big enough job for all of us, even with the help of the Higher Power. But later on we can practice self-discipline in other ways to keep a firm grip on our minds so that we don't start that old kind of thinking. If we daydream too much, we'll be in danger of reverting to old ways. *Am I now practicing self-discipline?*

MEDITATION FOR THE DAY

Concerning material things, you must rely on your own wisdom and that of others. In spiritual matters you cannot rely so much on your own wisdom as on God's guidance. In dealing with personalities, it is a mistake to step out too much on your own. You must try to be guided by God as you understand Him in all human relationships. You cannot accomplish much of value in dealing with people until God decides that you are ready. You alone do not have the power or wisdom to put things right between others. You must rely on God to help you in these vital matters.

PRAYER FOR THE DAY

I pray that I may rely on God in dealing with the problems of others. I pray that I may try to follow His guidance in all personal relationships.

One thing that keeps me rational is a sense of loyalty to the other members of my group. I know I'd be letting them down if I ever took a step backward again. When I was in turmoil, I wasn't loyal to anybody. I should have been loyal to my family, but I wasn't. I let them down by my disruptive behavior. When I came into this program, I found a group of people who not only were helping each other to recover but were loyal to each other by staying rational themselves. *Am I loyal to my group and this program?*

MEDITATION FOR THE DAY

Calmness is constructive of good; agitation is destructive of good. I should not rush into action. I should first be calm and seek guidance. Then I should act only as God directs me through my conscience. Faith and trust will keep me calm when all around me are agitated. Calmness is trust in action. I should seek all things that can help me cultivate calmness. To attain material things, the world learns to attain speed. To attain spiritual things, I must learn to attain a state of calm.

PRAYER FOR THE DAY

I pray that I may learn how to have inner peace. I pray that I may be calm so that God can work through me.

MAY 11 THOUGHT FOR THE DAY

We can depend on those members of the group who have gone all out for the program. They come to meetings. They work with other distressed people. They do not have recurring turmoil. They are loyal members. I am trying to be a loyal member of my group. When I am tempted to let my distress recur, I tell myself that if I did I'd be letting down the other members, who are the best friends I have. *Am I going to let them down if I can help it?*

MEDITATION FOR THE DAY

Wherever there is true fellowship and love between people, God's spirit is always there as the Divine Third. In all human relationships, the Divine Spirit is what brings them together. When a life is changed through the channel of another person, it is God, the Divine Third, who always makes the change, using the person as a means. The moving power behind all spiritual things, all personal relationships is God, the Divine Third, who is always there. No personal relationships can be entirely right without the presence of God's Spirit.

PRAYER FOR THE DAY

I pray that I may be used as a channel by God's spirit. I pray that I may feel that the Divine Third is always there to help me.

MAY 12   THOUGHT FOR THE DAY

When we come into this program looking for a way out of our turmoil, we really need a lot more than that. We need fellowship. We need to get the things that are troubling us out into the open. We find that we need a new outlet for our energies and a new strength beyond ourselves that will help us to face life instead of running from it. In this program we find the things that we need. *Have I found the things that I need in this program?*

MEDITATION FOR THE DAY

Turn out all thoughts of doubt and fear and resentment. Never tolerate them if you can help it. Bar the windows and doors of your mind against them as you would bar your home against a thief. What greater treasures can you have than faith and courage and love? All are stolen from you by doubt and fear and resentment. Face each day with hope and peace, which are the results of true faith in God.

PRAYER FOR THE DAY

I pray that I may feel protected and safe, and not only when I am sheltered. I pray that I may have protection and safety in the midst of the storms of life.

MAY 13   THOUGHT FOR THE DAY

In this program we find fellowship and release and strength. And when we find these things, the real reasons for our afflictions are taken away. The unrest, which was a symptom of underlying trouble, has no more justification in our minds. We no longer have need to fight against impending irrationality. This kind of threat just naturally leaves us. At first we are uncomfortable that we can't indulge ourselves, but in time we are glad that we don't have to experience affliction. *Am I glad that I don't have to suffer that distress any longer?*

MEDITATION FOR THE DAY

Try never to judge another or yourself. The human mind is so delicate, so complex that only God can know it wholly. Each mind is different, actuated by diverse motives, controlled by distinctive circumstances, influenced by varied sufferings. You cannot know all the influences that have gone to make up a personality. Therefore, it is impossible for you to judge that personality. Only God knows each person wholly and can change him. Leave to God the unraveling and reweaving of such mysteries.

PRAYER FOR THE DAY

I pray that I may not judge others. I pray that I may be certain that God can set right what is wrong in each of us.

MAY 14   THOUGHT FOR THE DAY

Having got over our affliction, we have only just begun to enjoy the benefits of this program. We find new friends, so that we are no longer lonely. We find new relationships with our families and others, so that we are happier at home. We find release from our past troubles and worries through a new way of looking at things. We find an outlet for our energies in helping other people. *Am I now enjoying these benefits of the program?*

MEDITATION FOR THE DAY

God sees what is within you as no man can see. Your reason for existence is to grow more and more toward the perfection of that Higher Power and to develop more and more His spirit within you. You can often see in others those qualities and aspirations which you yourself possess. Your motives and aspirations can be understood only by those who have attained the same spiritual level that you have.

PRAYER FOR THE DAY

I pray that I may not expect complete understanding from others. I pray that I may expect understanding only from God, as I try to grow more like Him.

MAY 15   THOUGHT FOR THE DAY

We find new strength and peace in the realization that there must be a Power greater than ourselves that is running the universe. It is a Power that is on our side when we live a good life. So this program really never ends. We begin by overcoming turmoil and go on from there to many new opportunities for happiness and usefulness. Each challenge and each accomplishment form a part of the new and growing strength. Each encounter brings greater peace. *Am I truly enjoying the ever-expanding ways in which this program augments my life?*

MEDITATION FOR THE DAY

We should seek first not material things but spiritual things. The material things will come to us as we honestly work for them. Many people seek the material things first and think they can then grow into knowledge of the spiritual realm. We cannot serve God and Mammon at the same time. Until we have honesty, purity, unselfishness, and love, quantities of material things are of little real use to us.

PRAYER FOR THE DAY

I pray that I may put much effort into acquiring spiritual things. I pray that I may not expect other rewards until I am right spiritually.

In the story of the Good Samaritan the traveler was beaten by robbers and left lying beside the road, half dead. A priest and a Levite passed by on the other side of the road. But the Good Samaritan was moved with compassion and sought to assist the traveler. He bound up his wounds and took him to an inn and cared for him. *Do I treat another as the priest and Levite did or as the Good Samaritan did?*

MEDITATION FOR THE DAY

Never weary in prayer. When one day you see how unexpectedly your prayer has been answered, then you will regret that you have prayed so little. Prayer changes things for you. Practice praying until your trust in a Higher Power has become strong. And then pray on because it has become so much a habit that you need it daily. Keep praying until prayer seems to become communion with God. That is the note on which true times of prayer should end.

PRAYER FOR THE DAY

I pray that I may form the habit of daily prayer. I pray that I may find the strength I need, as a result of this communion.

A lot of well-meaning people behave like the priest and the Levite in the story of the Good Samaritan. They pass by on the other side, scorning the sufferer, telling him how low he is, with no will power, no self-control. Yet he really has fallen before his problem in the same way the victim in the story fell before robbers. The member of our group who is working with others is like the Good Samaritan. *Am I moved with compassion to care for another suffering person?*

MEDITATION FOR THE DAY

I must constantly live in preparation for something better to come. All of life is a preparation for something better. I must anticipate the morning to come. I must feel in the night of sorrow that understanding joy, that confident expectation of better things to come. All of my existence in this world is a kind of training for a better life. "Sorrow may endure for a night, but joy cometh in the morning." So it has been in the night of my turmoil. God has something better in store if I make myself ready for it.

PRAYER FOR THE DAY

I pray that when life is over I will return to an eternal spaceless life with God. I pray that I may make this life a preparation.

MAY 18   THOUGHT FOR THE DAY

We are in this program for two main reasons: to stay rational ourselves and to help others gain the same rationality. It is well known that helping others is a part of staying rational yourself. It has also been proved that it is very hard to stay rational all by yourself. A lot of people have tried it and failed. They come to a few meetings and then stay rational alone for a few more months, but usually they eventually succumb to the old habits again. *Do I know that I can't stay rational all by myself?*

MEDITATION FOR THE DAY

Look through faith into that place beyond space or time where God dwells and whence you come and to which you will eventually return. To look beyond material things is within the power of everyone's imagination. Faith's look saves you from despair. Faith's look brings a peace beyond all understanding. Faith's look gives you a new and vital power and a wonderful peace and serenity.

PRAYER FOR THE DAY

I pray that I may have faith's look. I pray that by faith I may look beyond the now to eternal life.

MAY 19   THOUGHT FOR THE DAY

Fellowship is a big part of staying mentally stable. The doctors call it group therapy. We never go to a group meeting without taking something out of it with us. Sometimes we don't feel like going to a meeting, and we think of excuses to stay away. But we usually end up going anyway. And we get some lift out of every meeting we attend. These meetings are part of staying rational, and we get more out of a meeting if we try to contribute something to it. *Am I contributing my share at meetings?*

MEDITATION FOR THE DAY

"He brought me up out of a horrible pit, out of the miry clay, and set my feet upon a rock and established my goings." The first part, "He brought me up out of the horrible pit," means that, when I turned to a God of my understanding and put my problem in His hands, He helped me overcome my errors and temptations. "And set my feet upon a rock" means that, when I began to trust Him in all things, He gave me true security. "And established my goings" means that, when I honestly began to try to live the way God wants me to live, He gave me His guidance in my daily living.

PRAYER FOR THE DAY

I pray that my feet have been set upon a rock. I pray that I may rely on God to guide my comings and goings.

If we get up at a meeting and tell something about ourselves in order to help another person, we feel a lot better. It's the old law of the more you give the more you get. Witnessing and confession are part of staying rational. You never know when you may help someone. Helping others is one of the best ways to stay rational yourself. And the satisfaction you get from helping others is one of the finest experiences you can have. *Am I helping others?*

MEDITATION FOR THE DAY

Without God no real victory is ever won. All the military victories of great conquerors have passed into history. The real victories are won in the spiritual realm. The real victories are those over personal weakness and false ideals. They can lead to a victorious and abundant life. Keep a brave and trusting heart. Face all difficulties in the spirit of conquest. Remember that, where God is, there is the true victory.

PRAYER FOR THE DAY

I pray that the forces of evil in my life will flee before God's presence. I pray that with Him I may win the real victory over myself.

One of the finest things about this program is the sharing. Sharing is a wonderful way to do things, because the more you share the more you have. In our past days of turmoil we didn't do much, if any, sharing. We used to keep things to ourselves, partly because we were ashamed but mostly because we were selfish. And we were very lonely, because we didn't share. When we came into the program, the first thing we found was sharing. We heard others frankly sharing their experiences in courts, hospitals, jails, and arguments, and all the usual mess that goes with our kinds of problems. *Am I now sharing?*

MEDITATION FOR THE DAY

Character is developed by the daily discipline of duties done. Be obedient to the highest vision and take the straight way. Do not fall into the error of calling on God and then not doing the things that should be done. You need a life of prayer and meditation, but you must still do your work in life. The busy person is wise to rest, wait patiently for God's guidance, and then do what should be done.

PRAYER FOR THE DAY

I pray that I may be obedient to the heavenly vision. I pray that, if I fall, God will help me pick myself up and go on.

What impresses us most at a group meeting is the willingness to share without holding anything back. Soon we find ourselves sharing also. We begin telling our own experiences, and by so doing we help others. When we've got these things off our chest, we feel a lot better. It does us a lot of good to share with others who are in the same box that we were in. *Do I know that the more I share the better chance I'll have to stay rational?*

MEDITATION FOR THE DAY

Constantly claim the strength of the God of your understanding. Once you are convinced of the right of a course of action, once you are reasonably sure of God's guidance, claim that strength. You can claim all the strength you need to meet any situation. You can claim a new supply when your own is exhausted. You need not beg, for that belittles and delays. If you appropriate God's strength in a good cause, you draw upon it at once.

PRAYER FOR THE DAY

I pray that I may claim God's strength whenever I need it. I pray that I may live as a child of God.

The Twelfth Step of this program, working with others, can be subdivided into five words beginning with the letter *c*. These are *confidence, confession, conviction, conversion,* and *continuance*. The first step in trying to help others is to gain their confidence. We tell of our own experiences so that they will see that we know what we're talking about. They will realize that they are not alone and that others have had experiences as bad or worse. This gives them confidence that they can be helped. *Do I care enough about others to gain their confidence?*

MEDITATION FOR THE DAY

I failed not so much when tragedy happened as before the happening, by all the little things I might have done but did not do. I must prepare for the future by doing the right thing at the right time now. If a thing should be done, I should deal with that thing today and get it right with God before I allow myself to undertake any new task. I should look upon myself as performing God's errands. Then I should return to tell Him in quiet communion that the message was delivered or the task done.

PRAYER FOR THE DAY

I pray that I may seek no credit for the results of what I do. I pray that I may leave the outcome of my actions to God.

In Twelfth Step work the second part is confession. By frankly sharing with prospects, we get them talking about their own experiences. They will open up and confess things to us that they haven't been able to tell others. They feel better when this confession has been made. It's a great load off their minds, for the things that are kept hidden injure deeply. They feel a sense of release and freedom when they have opened up their hearts to us. *Do I care enough about others to help them make a confession?*

MEDITATION FOR THE DAY

I should help others all I can. I must never say that I have only enough strength for my own needs. The more I give away the more I will keep. What I keep only to myself I will lose in the end. As I grow, a greater strength will be given me. My circle of helpfulness will widen more and more. My reward is measured not by how well I am known but by my willingness to help those who do not know.

PRAYER FOR THE DAY

I pray that I may have a sincere willingness to give. I pray that I will not hold back for myself alone the strength I have received.

The third thing in Twelfth Step work is conviction. Prospects must be convinced that they honestly want help with their affliction. They must see and admit that their lives are unmanageable and face the fact that they must do something about their condition. They must be absolutely honest with themselves and face themselves as they really are. They must be convinced that they will have to give up their addictiveness, compulsion, obsession, whatever possesses them, and see that their whole lives depend on this. *Do I care enough about others to help them reach this conviction?*

MEDITATION FOR THE DAY

There is no limit to what you can accomplish in helping others. Keep that well in mind. Never relinquish any work or give up the thought of any accomplishment because it seems beyond your power. Only give it up if you feel that it is not God's work for you. The tiny seed underground has the capacity to break through solid rock or to grow around an obstacle to emerge. Even then there is no certainty that warmth and sunlight will greet it. None of these drawbacks stifle the seed or persuade it to abandon the effort.

PRAYER FOR THE DAY

I pray that I may never become discouraged in helping others. I pray that I will always rely on the power of God to help me persist.

In Twelfth Step work the fourth part is conversion. This means change. Prospects must learn to change their way of thinking. Until now everything they've done has been connected with confused feelings. Now they must face a new kind of life without irrationality. They must see and admit that they cannot overcome those distressing things by their own will power and must turn to a Higher Power for help. They try this and find that it works. *Do I care enough about others to help them make this conversion?*

MEDITATION FOR THE DAY

Discipline of yourself is absolutely necessary before the power of God is given to you. Do you see this discipline in others who manifest the power of God? Those people made themselves ready. All of life is a preparation, and when He knows that you are ready, God will endow you with those powers. Learn the spiritual laws and ward off failure.

PRAYER FOR THE DAY

I pray that I may manifest God's power in my daily living. I pray that I may discipline myself so as to be ready to meet every opportunity.

The fifth part of Twelfth Step work is continuance. This means staying with the prospects after they have started on the new way of living. We must stay with them and not let them down. We must encourage them to go to meetings regularly for fellowship and help. They will learn that staying rational is a lot easier in the fellowship of others who are trying to do the same thing. We can encourage them by seeing them, phoning, writing, and carrying out good sponsorship. *Do I care enough about others to continue as long as necessary?*

MEDITATION FOR THE DAY

We admire the flower but must be reminded of the root. There would be no blossom without the root. Nor would the flower last without a strong root. Both kinds of growth are necessary. The higher the growth upward the deeper must be the root. My life cannot flower unless it is rooted in faith.

PRAYER FOR THE DAY

I pray that my life may be deeply rooted in faith. I pray that I may feel deeply secure.

In this program we learn that since we are persons with afflictions we can be uniquely useful to others. We can help others in ways that those who have not had our experiences cannot. That makes us different, and ours is a unique group. We have taken our own greatest defeat, failure, and sickness to use as a means of helping others. We who have been there know the way. *Do I believe that I can be uniquely useful?*

MEDITATION FOR THE DAY

I should try to practice feeling the presence of God. I can feel that He is with me and near me, protecting and strengthening me. In spite of difficulty, trial, failure, the presence suffices. I should try to live as though God were beside me, though I cannot see Him. Were I made with that ability, there would be no need for faith. But I can feel His spirit with me.

PRAYER FOR THE DAY

I pray that I may practice the presence of God. I pray that by so doing I may never feel alone or helpless again.

Those of us who have learned to put our affliction in the hands of a Higher Power can help others to do so. We can be used as a connection between another's need and God's supply of strength. We in this program can be uniquely useful because we have had the misfortune and the fortune to be distressed ourselves. *Do I want to be a uniquely useful person? Will I use my own greatest defeats and failures as a weapon to help others?*

MEDITATION FOR THE DAY

I will try to help others. I will try not to let a day pass without reaching out a hand of love to someone. Each day I will try to do something to lift another human being out of the sea of discouragement into which he or she has fallen. My help is needed to raise the helpless to courage, to strength, to faith, to health. In my gratitude I will help lift a burden from another.

PRAYER FOR THE DAY

I pray that I may be used by God to lighten many burdens. I pray that many souls may be helped through my efforts.

I am a part of this program, one of many, but I am one. I need the program's principles for the development of the buried life within me. The group may be human in membership, but it is divine in its purpose. It points me toward God as I understand him and toward a better way of life. Participating in the privilege of the movement, I shall share in the responsibilities. I will accept my share of the load joyfully. If I fail, the group fails. If I succeed, the group succeeds. *Do I accept this as my credo in the program?*

MEDITATION FOR THE DAY

What does praising God really mean? It means being grateful for all the wonderful things in the universe and all the blessings in your life. In being grateful and humble, we have more power to vanquish wrongs than mere resignation. A grateful being has no time for temptation to do wrong. He is secure in knowing that fundamentally all is well.

PRAYER FOR THE DAY

I pray that I may be grateful for all my blessings. I pray that I may be humble because I know that those blessings are a gift to me from God.

I shall not wait to be drafted for service to the program. I shall volunteer. I shall be loyal in my attendance, generous in my giving, kind in my criticism, creative in my suggestions, and loving in my attitude. Whenever I am with my group, I shall give my interest, my enthusiasm, my devotion, and, most important, myself. *Do I also now accept this as a part of my credo?*

MEDITATION FOR THE DAY

Prayer is one form of meditation. It is sometimes a glance of faith or a look or word of love. Meditation is a feeling of confidence in the goodness and purpose in the universe. Like prayer, it gives us added strength to meet adversity and overcome it. If it clears our heads, helping us better to understand our need for and dependence upon God, then it is fruitful. Our existence is chained to our human limitations, but through meditation and prayer we transcend them to a point where we grasp a concept of a Supreme Being in our midst.

PRAYER FOR THE DAY

I pray that I may learn how to pray and to meditate. I pray that I may thus be linked to the will and mind of God.

JUNE 1 THOUGHT FOR THE DAY

Some things I do not miss since I have become more rational. I do not miss tremors, migraines, muscle cramps, depressive guilt, insomnia, rash talk, nausea, aching eyes. Facing others at breakfast when what they see spoils their appetite or disgusts them. Composing alibis and having to remember them. Trying to dress or shave with a hand that won't go where it should. Opening my billfold or purse to find it empty of funds. *I don't miss things like that, do I?*

MEDITATION FOR THE DAY

We were all born with a spark of the Divine in us. It had been all but smothered by the life we were living. That classic spark has to be tended and nurtured so that it will eventually grow into a real desire to live right. By trying to do the will of God, we grow more and more in the new way of life. The way of our transformation from the material to the spiritual is the way of Divine companionship.

PRAYER FOR THE DAY

I pray that I may tend the spark of the Divine within me so that it will grow. I pray that I may be gradually transformed from the old life to the new life.

JUNE 2   THOUGHT FOR THE DAY

Some of the things I do not miss since becoming more rational: I sometimes wondered if the car was in my garage or how I got home, if I was at home. I'd struggle to remember where I was, what had happened, if it was me or a dream. I'd surely like to get to work, if I could only remember where. *Am I positive I don't want any more of these things?*

MEDITATION FOR THE DAY

You cannot believe in a Higher Power and keep your selfish ways. The self shrivels up and dies. Upon the soul is stamped God's image. The elimination of selfishness in the growth of love is the goal of life. At first you have only a faint likeness of a Supreme Force, but the picture grows and takes on more and more intensity. It is the Light that fills the darkness of the world.

PRAYER FOR THE DAY

I pray that I may develop that faint likeness I have to the Divine. I pray that others may see in me some of the power of God's grace at work.

JUNE 3　　THOUGHT FOR THE DAY

More things I do not miss since becoming rational: Running all over town to find a drink, a fix, pills, an alibi. I used to meet someone and try to cover up that I felt truly animal. I'd look at myself in the mirror and recognize instantly the biggest idiot of all. The struggle to snap out of it seemed to drag on for days. I wondered if it would ever end. *Am I convinced that I really don't need or miss all those sick things in my life?*

MEDITATION FOR THE DAY

Love is the power that transforms your life. Try to love your friends, family, even strangers, and try to extend that love to yourself. Love for your Higher Power is the result of gratitude and is the acknowledgment of the blessing that He has given you. This love recognizes His gifts and leaves the way open for Him to shower yet more blessings on your thankful heart.

PRAYER FOR THE DAY

I pray that I may try to love God and all persons. I pray that I may continually thank Him for all His blessings.

JUNE 4   THOUGHT FOR THE DAY

Some things I find I like since becoming a more coherent person. I like feeling good in the morning. I like having full use of my intelligence and joy in the work I do. Not having to feel remorse, I find life a pleasant thing, not a threat. I have my friends' confidence and prospects for a happy future. Is there anything as inspiring as an appreciation for the simple beauties of life? I'm getting to know what things are really all about. *How could I want to exchange these things for what I had then?*

MEDITATION FOR THE DAY

Molding one's life means cutting and shaping the material into something good, which can express the spiritual. All material things are the clay out of which we mold something spiritual. We must first recognize the selfishness in our desires and motives, in our actions and words. Then we model and restyle it into a spiritual weapon for good. As the effort progresses, we see more clearly what must be done to mold life into something better.

PRAYER FOR THE DAY

I pray that I may mold my life into something useful and good. I pray that I may not be discouraged by the slow progress that I make and that God will give me persistence.

JUNE 5   THOUGHT FOR THE DAY

We afflicted persons are fortunate to be living in a time when there is such a thing as our program. Before that there was very little hope for anyone distressed as we were. The program is a great rebuilder of human wreckage. It takes people whose personality problems express themselves in distraught behavior and offers something that allows the recovery of rationality. It allows them to find a much better way of living. *Have I found a better way of living?*

MEDITATION FOR THE DAY

Very quietly our Higher Power speaks through our thoughts and feelings. If we listen, we will never be disappointed in the results in our lives. That voice can quell the unrest, and it evokes strength as well as tenderness. We come to rely upon it to learn the ways we may develop moral strength or self-fulfillment or restraint. Our receptivity is bounded only by a willingness to hear. Our entire lives are revitalized by that secret voice.

PRAYER FOR THE DAY

I pray that I may listen for the voice of God. I pray that I may obey the leading of my conscience.

JUNE 6   THOUGHT FOR THE DAY

Addiction, alcoholism, compulsions, excesses are all usually symptoms of some underlying personality problem. They are the ways we distressed persons express our particular difficulties with life. I believe that I was potentially irrational from the start. I had a feeling of inferiority or inadequacy. I didn't make friends easily, since there seemed to be a wall between me and other people. And I was lonely. I was not well adjusted to life. *Did I use turmoil to escape from myself and life?*

MEDITATION FOR THE DAY

According to the varying needs of each person, so does each person think of God. It is not necessary for you to think of the God of your understanding as others think of Him, but it is necessary that you know that He supplies what you personally need. The weak need God's strength. The strong need God's tenderness. The tempted and fallen need God's saving grace. The righteous need God's pity for sinners. The lonely need God as a friend. The fighters for righteousness need God as a leader. You may think of Him in any way that gives you comfort and strength.

PRAYER FOR THE DAY

I pray that I may think of God as supplying my needs. I pray that I will bring all problems to Him for help in meeting them.

JUNE 7   THOUGHT FOR THE DAY

Whatever our affliction, we can learn from others. Alcoholism, drug addiction, emotional excess, and other compulsions—all lead to turmoil. Each affliction seems to progress through stages: social conflict, troublesome habitual involvement, and finally chaos. Each is a progressive degeneration. Some of us end in jail, some in hospitals, some in court. Eventually most of us experience loss of job, home, family, friends, and always self-respect. Usually there are tragic outcomes—pain, suffering, death. *Have I made the choice to avoid the tragic outcomes?*

MEDITATION FOR THE DAY

You can live a new life. You can grow in grace, power, and beauty. Reach ever upward after the things of the spirit. As the seedling grows to reach the light, your character grows as you reach for the things of the spirit—for beauty, for love, for honesty, for purity, and for unselfishness.

PRAYER FOR THE DAY

I pray that I may reach upward. I pray that my character may alter as I reach for the things of the spirit.

JUNE 8   THOUGHT FOR THE DAY

Those with our affliction are never cured. The affliction is only arrested. No matter how long we have been rational, if we slip back again, we are as bad off or worse than ever. There is no exception to this rule in the history of this program. We can never recapture the few good times in the past. They are gone forever. *Have I learned in this program that I can never recapture anything of the old days but more misery?*

MEDITATION FOR THE DAY

Your life has been given to you mainly for the purpose of training your spirit. This life we live is not so much for the body as for the soul. We often choose the way of life that best suits the body, not the way that best suits the soul. God would have you choose what best suits both. Accept this belief, and a wonderful molding of character is the result. Reject it, and God's purpose is frustrated, and your spiritual progress is delayed. Your soul is being trained by the good you choose. Thus the purpose of your life is being accomplished.

PRAYER FOR THE DAY

I pray that I may choose what is good for my soul. I pray that I may realize God's purpose for my life.

JUNE 9 THOUGHT FOR THE DAY

After enough distress, enough turmoil, we finally hit bottom. We did not have to be financially broke, although many of us were. We were spiritually bankrupt, and we had a soul-sickness, a revulsion against ourselves and our disruptive way of living. Life had become impossible for us, and we had to end it or do something about it. Some of us didn't get all the way down. But when we'd had enough, the decision to climb back up faced us. *Am I glad now that I did something about it when I faced that decision?*

MEDITATION FOR THE DAY

Faith is not seeing but believing. We cannot perceive eternity but are chained to space and time. But our Higher Power is not confined within that limitation, and He, too, cannot be comprehended by our finite mind. If we try to merge our minds in a way to perceive His purposes, this oneness puts us in harmony with both God and others. The more we separate ourselves from that union, the greater our vulnerability to evil and our disharmony with God. Good comes from being in harmony with Him.

PRAYER FOR THE DAY

I pray that I may be in harmony with God. I pray that I may get into the stream of goodness in the universe.

If we have some moral, religious, or spiritual awareness from our past lives, we are better prospects for this program. When we reach bottom, at this crucial moment of total defeat, that prior awareness almost instinctively turns us to grasp whatever elements of faith are left. Whatever reserves of morality and faith are left deep in our hearts will rally to our help. *Have I had this spiritual consciousness?*

MEDITATION FOR THE DAY

Onlookers wonder when they see a person who can unexpectedly draw large sums of money from a bank for some emergency. But what they did not see were the countless small sums paid into that bank, earned from faithful work for a long period beforehand. So it is with the spirit. The world may see a person make a sudden demand on God's power, and that demand is met. The world doesn't see what that person has been putting in, in praises, thanksgivings, prayers, communion, small good deeds, faithfully and steadily over the years.

PRAYER FOR THE DAY

I pray that I may keep making deposits in God's bank. I pray that in my hour of need I may call upon these with assurance.

JUNE 11   THOUGHT FOR THE DAY

We distressed people have to believe in some Power greater than ourselves. We have to believe in a God of our own understanding. Not to believe in a Higher Power drives us to atheism, which is blind faith in the strange proposition that this universe originated in a cipher and aimlessly rushes nowhere. We turn to the Divine Principle, which gives us meaning as persons. *Have I stopped trying to be my own universe, running my own life?*

MEDITATION FOR THE DAY

Now that we are no longer afraid to think again, we learn that we are also not confined in what or how we think. I look back at life and realize how very little I was able to influence the things I desired and revered most. Now sometimes these are attained, and I marvel how, in the face of all my failings, my deficiencies, I can lay claim to them. I notice something else, too — that when I attain a desired thing, I am worthy in my own eyes. I seek little, but am humble and wait. In forcing the search, I was blind, but when not forcing the search, I am given sight.

PRAYER FOR THE DAY

I pray that today I may have inner peace. I pray that today I may be at peace with the world.

JUNE 12   THOUGHT FOR THE DAY

When we came into this program, we made a tremendous discovery. We found that we were sick persons rather than moral lepers. We were not such queer birds as we had thought. We found other people who had the same affliction that we had, who had been through the same experiences that we had been through. They had recovered. If they could do it, we could do it. *Was hope born in me the day I entered this program?*

MEDITATION FOR THE DAY

In a very short time after beginning the meditative habit, we begin learning how imperative it is that we build our house upon rock, through depending on a Higher Power and developing faith. When we build a life upon obedience to God and doing His will as we recognize or perceive it, you and I will become steadfast in trials, tribulations, and hardships.

PRAYER FOR THE DAY

I pray that my life may be founded upon the rock of faith. I pray that I may be obedient to the heavenly vision.

JUNE 13   THOUGHT FOR THE DAY

In this program we have to re-educate our minds. We have to learn to think differently. We have to take a long view of our affliction instead of a short view. We have to look through the moment to what lies beyond. We have to look through the night to the morning after. No matter how vital that brief outburst seems from the short view, we must learn that in the long run it is disaster for us. *Have I learned to look through the momentary turmoil to the better life that lies ahead?*

MEDITATION FOR THE DAY

If you are honestly trying to live the way you believe God wants you to live, you can get guidance from Him in times of meditation, provided your thoughts are directed toward learning His will. The attitude that greatly helps is subordinating your will to His, for that leads to far better control of life. As your impulses become less your own and more the enactment of God's spirit, you enhance the likelihood of deriving answers to many of life's questions.

PRAYER FOR THE DAY

I pray that I may try to think God's thoughts after the manner of His teachings. I pray that I may be guided by His thoughts.

JUNE 14 THOUGHT FOR THE DAY

In this program we learn that our affliction is our greatest enemy. Although we used to think that some aspects of the turmoil were our friends, the time came when they became our enemy. We don't know when this happened, but we know that it did. We began to get into trouble—hospitals, jail, courts, economic worries. We realize now that these excesses are our enemy. *Is it still my main challenge to stay rational?*

MEDITATION FOR THE DAY

It is not your circumstances that need altering so much as yourself. After you have changed, conditions will naturally change. Spare no effort to become all that God would have you become. Follow every good leading of your conscience. Take each day with no backward look. Face the day's problems with Him and seek his help and guidance in what you should do in every situation that may arise. Never look back. Never leave until tomorrow the thing that you are guided to do today.

PRAYER FOR THE DAY

I pray that God will help me to become all that He would have me be. I pray that I may face today's problems with good grace.

JUNE 15   THOUGHT FOR THE DAY

In this program we have three things: fellowship, faith, and service. Fellowship is wonderful, but its wonder lasts just so long. Then gossip, disillusionment, and boredom may enter in. Worry and fear come back at times, and we find that fellowship is not the whole story. Then we need faith. When we are alone, with nobody to pat us on the back, we must turn to God for help. *Can I say, "Thy will be done," and mean it?*

MEDITATION FOR THE DAY

We sometimes wonder if we can do as much to help ourselves as others tell us we can. Perhaps we are being hesitant to accept challenge, reluctant to face things that we have hitherto failed to face. There are some circumstances that can be modified and some that will never change through what we can do. If we know that we're powerless over our affliction, we can accept also that we are sometimes just as powerless over life situations beyond our capacity to change. We must be honest, however, in recognizing that at some later time we may be able to deal effectively with these now-unyielding problems. We need to seek the help of a Higher Power to give us that capacity.

PRAYER FOR THE DAY

I pray that I may have the courage to change the things in my life that I can change. I pray that I will be guided by God's wisdom in doing so.

Even faith is not the whole story. There must be service. We must give our recovery away if we want to keep it. A part of the cure, it is often said, is to know that you have the disease. Some persons fail to realize this, but if we help someone who asks for our assistance, we can show how we came to know about such turmoil and what it has been like since we came into this program. When we do so, we help ourselves as much as the prospect. *Am I convinced that I must give away my experience with recovery in order to keep its benefits?*

MEDITATION FOR THE DAY

Good habits can be formed, just as bad habits can be formed. We learn by trying that meditation is most effective early in the day, before life crowds us with distracting events. With a quiet, reassuring confidence we gain the calm, serene hold on things that can effectively insulate us through the day from forces that might otherwise create real problems. We seek communion with our Higher Power in that early moment just as we do when the world's struggles become overpowering. We develop the habit of meditation.

PRAYER FOR THE DAY

I pray that I may not let God be crowded out of my life. I pray that I may seek Him early in the day, every day.

We in this program have the privilege of living two lives in one lifetime, one life of affliction, failure, and defeat and another life of rationality, peace of mind, and usefulness. We who have recovered our sanity are modern miracles. And we're living on borrowed time. Some of us might have been dead long ago, but we have been given another chance to live. *Do I owe a debt of gratitude to this program that I can never repay as long as I live?*

MEDITATION FOR THE DAY

Directing our thoughts to the influence of a Power greater than ourselves gives us a lifeline that is vital in dispelling oppressive environments that impinge upon us. The thought of God banishes loneliness, summons help to conquer our faults. As we become more spiritually oriented, we tend to be less engaged by materialistic involvements. The influence of a Higher Power will endure when all else disintegrates.

PRAYER FOR THE DAY

I pray that I may think of God often. I pray that I may rest in peace, knowing of His love and will to guide me.

The way of living of this program is not an easy one. But it's an adventure in living that is really worthwhile. And it's so much better than our old chaotic way that there is no comparison. Our lives without the program would be worth nothing. With the program we have a chance to live reasonably good lives. It's worth the battle no matter how hard the going is from day to day. *Isn't it worth the effort to keep what I've discovered?*

MEDITATION FOR THE DAY

We never completely escape the temptations of life. We have to acknowledge that most of our choices have been our own, without the guidance of a Power greater than ourselves. That way has led us to grievous suffering many times. As we reflect upon this, we see how profoundly our behavior changes once a Higher Power begins to influence our lives. Through faith and trust we come to know a kind of impenetrable shield against those temptations that once were our undoing. They have not grown weak, but we have become strong through God's help.

PRAYER FOR THE DAY

I pray that I may grow stronger from my relationship with God. I pray that I may pass on my strength to the persons I seek to help.

JUNE 19 THOUGHT FOR THE DAY

We have a choice every day of our lives. We can take the path that leads to turmoil and even death. But our next experience with a drug, alcohol, an emotional crisis, or a compulsive indulgence may be the last one. We can also take the path that leads to a reasonably happy and useful life. The program we follow shows the way, and the choice is ours each hour of each day. This is the path we have been on. *Will it be the path I choose today?*

MEDITATION FOR THE DAY

The real work in life is to grow spiritually. To do so we must follow the path of diligently seeking good. The hidden wonders of the spirit are revealed by search. It is a steady progression from one point to the next, ever ascending in rewards. Work on the material plane must be secondary to one's real lifework. The necessary material things are those that help us attain the spiritual life. We cannot become buried in an overaccumulation of the former, which smothers the latter.

PRAYER FOR THE DAY

I pray that I may keep growing spiritually. I pray that I may make this my real lifework, which I strive to give to others as well.

You should be ready and willing to carry the message of this program when called upon to do so. Live for some purpose greater than yourself. Each day there is something more to work for. You have received so much already that you should have a vision that gives your life a direction. You should have a purpose that adds meaning to each new day. The purpose is for something greater than ourselves. *What is my purpose for this day?*

MEDITATION FOR THE DAY

Since so much of what we expect of ourselves in the working of our twelve steps is motivated by faith and based upon trust, we have won major ground merely in starting. We are this far. Our Higher Power will assuredly do for us what He has so steadfastly done for all those we see around us. In a few months the changes in some are unbelievable. Each person recovered is a miracle and a monument to God's unfailing promises to those who will accept Him.

PRAYER FOR THE DAY

I pray that I may see God with the eyes of faith. I pray that this will produce the miracle of change in me that is so imperative.

Intelligent faith in that Power greater than ourselves can be counted on to stabilize our emotions, our addictions, our compulsions, our turmoils. It has an incomparable capacity to help us look at life in a balanced perspective. We look up, around, and away from ourselves, and we see that nine out of ten things which at the moment upset us will shortly disappear. Problems solve themselves, criticism and unkindness vanish as though they had never existed. *Have I got the proper perspective toward life?*

MEDITATION FOR THE DAY

A truly spiritual person would like to have a serene mind. The only way to keep calm and rational in this troubled society is to have deep inward serenity. The person thus equipped sees spiritual things as the true realities and material things as fleeting. Such peace is not obtained by reasoning, since reasoning is limited by the concepts of time and space. What we read comes from minds equally limited. Only by an act of faith, a venture into belief, is it possible to acquire God's serenity and calmness.

PRAYER FOR THE DAY

I pray that I may look up, around, and away from myself. I pray that I may acquire peace and serenity, even in the midst of great turmoil or in dealing with the turmoil of others.

This program makes one fact clear—that the most imperative step we must take, after acknowledging our powerlessness, is to seek a Higher Power. Sometimes we find that in coming to know a God of our understanding we gain the amazing power to begin to cope with affliction. Before that we were so vulnerable. We opened the doors wide to recurring disaster, until a Power greater than ourselves stepped in. *Am I now allowing God to manage what I could not control?*

MEDITATION FOR THE DAY

Being human is sometimes an embarrassing and awkward thing. We seem to be pitifully uncertain, filled with specters of fear and failure. Difficulties arise at the slightest provocation. We wonder if we can ever win anything at all. How human to measure success only in terms of gain. How foolish not to measure success in the sunrise, our very existence, and miraculous changes in others. It is more meaningful to embrace God's measure, through faith, meditation, and trust.

PRAYER FOR THE DAY

I pray that I may face the future with courage. I pray that I may be given the strength to face human awkwardness and weakness steadily.

JUNE 23   THOUGHT FOR THE DAY

Rarely does a chain break in a strong link. Only the weak links fail. If we fail this day-by-day program, it will likely be where we are weakest. To be more steadfast, we emphasize constant contact with our Higher Power. Intelligent faith in His power can be counted on to help us master ourselves. If we had been that strong, we would not need to be in this program. There is no way we can compromise our entire dependence upon a Power greater than ourselves. *Do I still have secret thoughts that I am in complete control of myself?*

MEDITATION FOR THE DAY

You need to be constantly recharged by the power of the spirit of God. Commune with Him in these quiet moments until that Divine serenity flows into your own being and revives the weakened will. When you are weary, it is time to rest. When you hunger, it is time to eat. When your spirit wanes, it is time to seek God. Our worries, fears, concerns give way to His loving consciousness and abounding faith.

PRAYER FOR THE DAY

I pray that when I am weak I may always seek God's endless source of strength. I pray that in being thus revitalized I may meet the day's challenges.

Uncontrolled emotions are often our weakness. There may be other problems, too. The origin of such problems can be largely attributed to some form of instability. We suffer from conflicts from which we try to escape. Usually that means an outlet of some sort, in which we also lack control. We try through escapes to push away from realities we do not want to face. We borrow relief at a time of distress, but in so doing we rob the future of that time when relief would have come naturally. *If I take from the future to get something now, do I realize that I'm only short-changing myself in the long run?*

MEDITATION FOR THE DAY

When I let personal piques and resentments interfere with what I know to be proper conduct, I'm running contrary to God's plan of things. This leads to tearing down what I have sought His help in building. When I have no clear guidance from God, I must proceed the best I can on faith. The role of quiet faith will receive its reward as surely as acting upon God's direct guidance

PRAYER FOR THE DAY

I pray that I may not let myself become too upset. I pray that I will go quietly along the path of faith I have chosen.

JUNE 25   THOUGHT FOR THE DAY

One of the most encouraging facts of life is that our weaknesses can become our greatest assets. The challenge is considerable, for the first thing we must be able to do is think it possible. Many of us are easily discouraged, but if we are as willing to try to meet this challenge as we were to come into the program, we have already acquired a will to succeed. *Am I willing to change my weaknesses into my greatest assets?*

MEDITATION FOR THE DAY

Inasmuch as we are human, we find that our needs can usually be fulfilled to the degree that we work for them. Our spiritual needs are not of this kind, however. We develop a habit of daily maintenance of the spiritual life. We can augment this habit by seeking other ways to commune with God. Our practice here is meditation, but we can also pray each day. Sometimes we further build our spiritual lives by helping others as witnesses or sponsors. Each way advances our contact with our Higher Power and gives us greater faith on which to build.

PRAYER FOR THE DAY

I pray that I may accept the limitless and eternal Spirit. I pray that this guidance may help me to be useful to myself and others.

We must know the nature of our weakness before we can determine how to deal with it. When we are honest about its presence, we may discover that it is imaginary and can be overcome by a change of mental attitude. By keeping foremost in mind that our weakness is an illness, we can take the necessary steps to arrest it. As long as we do not deceive ourselves about the true nature of our affliction, we can take the necessary steps to arrest it. *Have I fully accepted the nature of my illness?*

MEDITATION FOR THE DAY

There is a proper time for everything. We must learn not to do things at the wrong time. It is always a temptation to do something immediately, instead of waiting until the proper moment. Timing is important. So many lives lack timing and balance. In times of crisis we can ask God's guidance so that we will not rush into action without thinking.

PRAYER FOR THE DAY

I pray that I may delay action until I feel that I am doing the right thing. I pray that I may not rush into things hastily.

JUNE 27   THOUGHT FOR THE DAY

If you can take troubles as they come, if you can maintain your calm and composure amid pressing duties, you have discovered a priceless secret of daily living. Then even if you must go through life weighed down by some inescapable misfortune, you have succeeded where most people have failed. *Have I achieved poise and peace of mind in my daily routine?*

MEDITATION FOR THE DAY

Take a blessing with you wherever you go. As you have been blessed, so bless others. Such stores of blessings are awaiting you in the months and years that lie ahead. Pass on your blessings. Shed a little blessing in the heart of one person, who is cheered to pass it on to another. So God's vitalizing, joy-giving message travels on.

PRAYER FOR THE DAY

I pray that I may pass on my blessings. I pray that they may flow into the lives of others.

You can prove to yourself that the meaning of life is basically and essentially an inner attitude. Try to remember what troubled you most a week ago. You will probably find it difficult to remember at all. With faith you can change attitudes, and with changed attitudes toward problems you are relieved of their burden. There is no need to face difficulties with fear or misgiving. *Have I changed my mental attitude?*

MEDITATION FOR THE DAY

You cannot see the future. It is a blessing that you cannot, for you likely could not bear to know all of it. That is why God only reveals it to you one day at a time. The first step each day is to lay your will before Him as an offering, ready for Him to do what He will for you. The second step is to be confident that God is powerful enough to do anything He wills. No miracle in human lives is impossible for Him. You are, after all, living proof of it. Ours is the present, and we leave the future to God.

PRAYER FOR THE DAY

I pray that I may gladly leave my future in God's hands. I pray that I may be confident that good things will happen as long as I am on the right path.

This program involves a continuous striving for improvement. There can be no long resting period. We must try to work at it all the time. We must constantly bear in mind that it is a program not to be measured in years. As members we never fully reach our goals, nor are we ever cured. Our past affliction is kept in abeyance only by daily living of the program. It is a timeless program in every sense. *Am I always aware that I live the program today and strive for improvement continuously?*

MEDITATION FOR THE DAY

Life is said to be a preparation for something better to come. Our Higher Power has a plan for our lives, and it will work out if we try to do as He wills. This is a time for discipline and prayer. The time for expression will come later. Life can be flooded through and through with joy and gladness. Prepare yourself for those better things to come. If that means living with adversity from time to time, we must surely do so. The hardship will pass, but our preparation continues.

PRAYER FOR THE DAY

I pray that I may prepare myself for better things that God has in store for me. I pray that I may trust Him for the governance of the future.

We were unable or unwilling during our enslavement to affliction to live in the present. The result was that we lived in a constant state of remorse and fear. This was attributed to the ungodly past and its morbid attractions or to the uncertain future and its vague forebodings. Now the only real hope for each of us is to face the present. Now is the time. This moment is ours, since the past is beyond recall. The future is as uncertain as life itself. Only the now belongs to us. *Am I certain I am living in the now, today?*

MEDITATION FOR THE DAY

I must forget the past as much as possible. The past is over and gone forever. Nothing can be done about the past except to make what restitution I can. I must not carry the burden of my past failures. I must go on in faith. The clouds will clear, and the way will lighten. The path will become less stony and obstructed with every forward step I take. I will heal from the bruises I suffered when I stumbled. My life will be made whole again, for God has no reproach when He has healed me.

PRAYER FOR THE DAY

I pray that I may not carry the burden of the past. I pray that I may cast it off and press on in faith.

JULY 1   THOUGHT FOR THE DAY

In following this program with its twelve steps, we have the advantage of a better understanding of our problems. Day after day our new rationality results in the formation of new habits, normal habits. As each twenty-four-hour period ends, we find that the business of staying rational is much less trying and fearsome. The ordeal is not as awesome as it seemed to be at first. *Do I find it easier to be rational day by day as I go along?*

MEDITATION FOR THE DAY

Learn daily the lesson of trust and calm in the midst of the storm of life. Whatever of sorrow or difficulty the day may bring, God's command to you is the same. Be grateful, humble, calm, and loving toward all people. Leave each soul better off for having met you or heard you. For all kinds of people this should be your attitude: a loving desire to help and an infectious spirit of calmness and trust in God. You have the answer to loneliness and fear, which is calm faith in the goodness and purpose in the universe.

PRAYER FOR THE DAY

I pray that I may be calm in the midst of storms. I pray that I may pass on this calmness to those who are lonely and full of fear.

JULY 2   THOUGHT FOR THE DAY

In the association with members of this group we have the advantage of the sincere friendship and understanding of the other members. Through social and personal contact we escape our old haunts and environments. This helps to remove the occasions of irrational suggestion. We find in this association a sympathy and a willingness of members to do everything in their power to help us. *Do I appreciate the wonderful fellowship of my group?*

MEDITATION FOR THE DAY

"Except ye become as little children, ye shall not enter the kingdom of heaven." All who seek heaven on earth or in the hereafter should become like children. In seeking things of the spirit, we should try to become childlike. Even as we grow older, the years of seeking can give us the attitude of the trusting child. We have the child's simple trust, joy in life, ready laughter, lack of criticism, and desire to share. We divest ourselves of the corroding influences of distrust and the cynicism of age.

PRAYER FOR THE DAY

I pray that I may become like a child in faith and hope. I pray that I may be like a child in friendliness and trust.

JULY 3   THOUGHT FOR THE DAY

At the beginning of this program there were only a few members. Now there are many groups and hundreds, even thousands, of members. True, the surface has been only scratched. There are probably millions of persons who desperately need this program. More and more people are making a start in it each day. One part of our recovery is making contact with some of those still in the blind alley of irrationality. We do not need to feel threatened, however, for it is no longer our chosen environment. *Do I believe that I can help others to find this program without feeling threatened myself?*

MEDITATION FOR THE DAY

"Blessed are they that hunger and thirst after righteousness, for they shall be filled." Only in the fullness of faith can the heartsick, faint, and weary be satisfied, healed, and rested. Think of the wonderful revelations still to be found by those who are trying to live the spiritual life. Much of life is spiritually unexplored country. Only to the consecrated and loving people who walk with God in spirit can these great discoveries be revealed.

PRAYER FOR THE DAY

I pray that I may not be held back by the material things of the world. I pray that I may walk with God in spirit.

JULY 4 THOUGHT FOR THE DAY

We celebrate our own independence this day, and each day from the time we come into this program. No greed for gain, no fees, no thought of profit, no political allegiances. What we rejoice about is our returned rationality and regeneration as persons able to live normal lives. The things we accomplish for ourselves and others come from the Higher Power and twelve basic steps. *Am I rejoicing today for my independence from turmoil and distress?*

MEDITATION FOR THE DAY

What is sometimes termed conversion in religion is often the discovery of God as a friend during time of need. What is sometimes termed religion is the experiencing of the help and strength of God's power in our lives. As He becomes our friend, we become friends to others. We experience true human friendship, and from this experience we can realize that God is our miracle-working Friend.

PRAYER FOR THE DAY

I pray that I may think of God as a Great Friend in time of need. I pray that I may follow Him wherever He leads me.

JULY 5   THOUGHT FOR THE DAY

Until we came into this program, most of us had tried desperately to "cure" our excesses. We were filled with the delusion that we could indulge them as our friends did without harm. We tried time and again to take it or leave it, but we could do neither. We always lapsed into ceaseless misery. Those closest to us threw up their hands in hurt bewilderment, in despair, and finally in disgust. We wanted to control ourselves. We realized that every reason to justify our actions was only a crazy excuse. *Have I given up every excuse for such turmoil?*

MEDITATION FOR THE DAY

Many things can upset you, and you can easily get off course. But remember that the Higher Power is near you all the time, ready to help if you call. You cannot forever hold out against God's will for you, nor can you upset God's plan for your life. It may be postponed by your willfulness and deliberate choice of evil. But a whole world of men and women cannot change God's laws or His purpose for the universe.

PRAYER FOR THE DAY

I pray that I may try to steer a straight course. I pray that I may accept God's direction in my life's journey.

JULY 6 THOUGHT FOR THE DAY

We tried to study our problem, wondering what was the cause of this strange affliction. Many of us underwent treatment, hospitalization, even confinement in institutions. In each case the relief was only temporary. We tried through crazy excuses to convince ourselves that we knew why we were irrational, but we went on regardless. Finally irrationality had gone beyond habit. We had become people who were destroying themselves against their own wills. *Am I completely free from my irrationality?*

MEDITATION FOR THE DAY

Never let yourself think that you cannot do something useful, that you never will be able to accomplish a useful task. The fact is that you can do practically anything in the field of human relationships if you are willing to call on God's supply of strength. It may not be immediately available, because you may not be entirely ready to receive it. But it will surely come when you are prepared for it. As you grow spiritually, you will be able to accomplish many useful things.

PRAYER FOR THE DAY

I pray that I may claim God's supply of strength by my faith in Him. I pray that it shall be given to me according to my faith.

JULY 7   THOUGHT FOR THE DAY

We had become hopelessly sick people—physically, emotionally, and spiritually. The power that controlled us was greater than ourselves. Many of us have said, "I hadn't gone that far. I hadn't lost my job. I still had my family; I stayed out of jail or the hospital." We made fools of ourselves, but we still thought we could control our affliction. *If I was one of those, have I fully changed my mind?*

MEDITATION FOR THE DAY

Painful as the present time may be, you will one day see the reason for it. You will see that it was a preparation for the lifework you are to do. Have faith that your prayers and aspirations will someday be answered. They may be answered in a way that seems painful to you but is the only right way. Selfishness and pride often make us want things that are not good for us. They need to be burned out of our natures. We must be rid of the blocks that are holding us back before we can expect our prayers to be answered.

PRAYER FOR THE DAY

I pray that I may be willing to go through a time of preparation. I pray that I may trust God for the outcome.

JULY 8   THOUGHT FOR THE DAY

Group members can tell you that they can look back and clearly see they were out of control long before they finally admitted it. Every one of us has gone through that stage when we wouldn't admit that we were out of control. It takes a lot of punishment to convince us, but one thing is certain. We all know from actual experience that when it comes to dishing out punishment our affliction has no equal. *Have I any reservations about being the kind of person who needs this program?*

MEDITATION FOR THE DAY

There is a force for good in the world, and when you are cooperating with that force for good, then good things happen to you. You have free will, the choice to be on the side of right or on the side of wrong. The force for good we call God's will. God has a purpose for the world, and He has a purpose for your life. He can work only through persons whose wills are His will. Be in the stream of goodness, and you will be on God's side.

PRAYER FOR THE DAY

I pray that I may try to make God's will my will. I pray that I may keep in the stream of goodness in the world.

JULY 9 THOUGHT FOR THE DAY

Disillusionment and spiritual confusion mark our age. Many of us have cast aside old ideas without acquiring new ones. Many men and women are creeping through life on their hands and knees, merely because they refuse to rely on any power but themselves. Many of them feel that they are being brave and independent, but actually they are only courting disaster. Anxiety and the inferiority complex have become the two greatest of all mental plagues. In this program we have an answer to these ills. *Have I ceased to rely on myself only?*

MEDITATION FOR THE DAY

Doubt and disenchantment spoil life. The doubting ones are the disenchanted ones. When you are in doubt, you are on the fence. You are not going anywhere, for doubt poisons all actions. You must learn to meet life with an affirmative attitude. There is good in the world, and we can follow that good. Power is available to help us do the right thing. Therefore, we must accept that power. We will accept the miracles of change we see in people's lives as evidence of God's power.

PRAYER FOR THE DAY

I pray that I will not be paralyzed by doubt. I pray that I may meet life affirmatively on the venture of faith.

We in this program do not enter into theological discussions, but, in carrying the message, we attempt to explain the simple "how" of the spiritual life: how faith in a Higher Power can help you overcome loneliness, fear, and anxiety; how it can help you get along with others; how it can make it possible for you to rise above pain, sorrow, and despondency; how it can help you overcome desires for things that destroy. *Do I have a simple, effective faith?*

MEDITATION FOR THE DAY

Expect miracles of change in people's lives. Do not be held back by disbelief. People can be changed, and they are often ready and waiting to be changed. Never believe that human nature cannot be altered. We see changed persons every day, and miracles of change happen daily in people's lives. If you have the faith that such changes are possible, you can be a channel for God's strength to alter the lives of others.

PRAYER FOR THE DAY

I pray that I may have the faith to expect miracles. I pray that I may be used by God to help change the lives of others.

JULY 11 THOUGHT FOR THE DAY

Our group does not try to chart the path for the human soul or lay out a blueprint of the workings of faith. We do tell the new member that we have renewed our faith in a Higher Power. In telling him, our faith is further renewed. We believe that faith is always close at hand, waiting for those who will listen to the spirit. We believe that there is a force for good and that, if we are linked with it, we are carried onward to a new life. *Am I persuaded that my faith and spiritual effort are vital parts of my recovery?*

MEDITATION FOR THE DAY

There is protection for you against the forces of evil. You can face all things through the power of God, which strengthens you. Part of your failure to overcome disruptive forces in the past was a lack of contact with the only real power that could sustain you. If you realize this now and benefit from your own observation of others about you who have changed as you will change, then you can feel assured that you also have the protection of the Higher Power. As we invoke His blessing upon you, so will you invoke His blessing upon those yet to come.

PRAYER FOR THE DAY

I pray that I may rely on God as I go through this new day. I pray that I may feel deeply secure, no matter what happens to me.

JULY 12   THOUGHT FOR THE DAY

Today is ours. Let us live today as we believe we ought to live it. Each day will have a new pattern that we cannot foresee. If weeks go by that we do not find solutions to each day's riddles, we are in trouble. We ask one question after another and find answers, one after another. We read the steps, go to meetings, call someone. We take part in the things we are avoiding and get honest about them. We put the emphasis on things as they should be, and not on appearances or the other mistaken ideas of the past. *Am I doing something now about protecting my hard-won rationality?*

MEDITATION FOR THE DAY

If you believe that God's grace has saved you, then you must believe that He would save you again, if necessary, and would keep you in the way you should go. Even a human rescuer does not save another person only to place him in other dangerous circumstances. Our Higher Power will willingly rescue body and soul, protecting us from all forces that might try thereafter to endanger us. God completes the task He sets out to do, as long as we retain faith.

PRAYER FOR THE DAY

I pray that I may trust God to keep me in the path I must walk. I pray that I may rely on Him to guide me.

JULY 13   THOUGHT FOR THE DAY

Before we came into this program, each of us was "flying blind." But the program gives us a directional beam to follow. As long as we keep on this heading, the signal of rationality keeps coming through, loud and clear. If we stray off course, we lose the signal. Unless we regain that signal, we are in real danger of flying blind again, crashing against the mountain of despair. *Am I sure that I can now stay on course?*

MEDITATION FOR THE DAY

Be expectant. Constantly expect better things. Believe that what your Higher Power has in store for you is better than anything you ever had before. The way to grow old happily is to expect better things right up to the end of your life and beyond. A good life is a growing life, with ever-widening horizons. There will evolve an ever-greater circle of friends and acquaintances and an ever-greater opportunity for usefulness.

PRAYER FOR THE DAY

I pray that I may await with complete faith the next good thing in store for me. I pray that I may always keep an expectant attitude toward life.

JULY 14 THOUGHT FOR THE DAY

One of the best things about this program is the peace of mind and serenity that it can bring. Before, we had no mental peace and no chance for it. We lived in a continuum of turmoil, caused by personal suffering, physical problems, and all manner of distractions. The loneliness, sense of inferiority, deception, and remorse were further torments. *In my days of recovery have I been freed to acquire peace of mind?*

MEDITATION FOR THE DAY

Try to find the ways in which your new-found spiritual life is helping you improve personal relationships. This new way of coping with things enters into all aspects of your life-style. Have you noticed that you deify material things less often? Do you have a keener awareness of the personality of a person you talk to? Do you tend to think about how you can help someone with a situation rather than how that person might help you? You are slowly changing into a better person. If you don't see these things, don't be concerned, for it is evident to others. Just now, what you see is the lack of conflict, the lack of hostility, the lack of avoidance by others.

PRAYER FOR THE DAY

I pray that God will continue to show me how I may progress in my spiritual development. I pray that I may learn more ways to help others.

JULY 15 THOUGHT FOR THE DAY

After we had stabilized through working this program, we gradually began to gain peace of mind and a serenity that we never thought were possible. This peace is based on a feeling that fundamentally all is well. That does not mean that all is well on the surface of things. Little things can keep going wrong, and big things can keep on upsetting us, too. But deep down we know that everything is eventually going to be all right, now that we are living sensible lives. *Have I achieved a deep serenity and peace of mind?*

MEDITATION FOR THE DAY

We are climbing a ladder in life. The climb is not easy for some of us. Some ladders seem to sink into the mire as we try to climb. Some ladders are not resting against anything but balance precariously in mid-air. A few rest on only one rail and easily skid. Some have only a few rungs intact. Sometimes we undertake a thing that seems impossible to achieve. Then we need to follow certain basic steps, make certain vital commitments, and proceed with a will to achieve. Our Higher Power provides us with this will, through faith.

PRAYER FOR THE DAY

I pray that I may climb the ladder of life without fear. I pray that I may progress steadily through the rest of my life with faith and confidence.

Our group is a place of fellowship where we learn to share each other's inner feelings. It is a privilege to belong and a duty to attend. Nowhere else can we find the bonds of friendship we find here. Our responsibilities to each other come from willing offering, not from obligation or with reluctance. We do not divide the group into cliques, professions, or any other artificial divisions. We are beings sharing the same afflictions. We devote our lives to the same goals and look to the same Higher Power. *Am I free of the subtle discrimination which can erode the unity of a group?*

MEDITATION FOR THE DAY

In times of personal adversity an increased sensitivity can evolve within us. Sometimes we lose our sense of proportion, for a simple thing can be magnified into something sinister. We must remain keenly aware of the facts. Since this greater intensity of perception offers some advantage as well as some hazard, we must learn to sort one from the other. We can greatly increase our ability to make right choices by reducing our degree of confusion. Trust in our Higher Power affords the serene and calming influence we need in these moments.

PRAYER FOR THE DAY

I pray that, whatever personal trials I may face, the hand of God will be there to lead me in the right way. I pray that I may follow Him serenely and calmly.

JULY 17   THOUGHT FOR THE DAY

The new life of rationality I am learning to live in this program is slowly making strides. I am beginning to get some of the deep peace of mind that I never thought possible. At first I doubted that it could happen, but after some time I sense that it is present. I try to live the program, for I believe what others described to me about reluctance and nonparticipation. I take the program seriously day by day. And I can see how this progress shows in the lives of others who do the same thing. *Will I continue to search for signs of progress in myself and others?*

MEDITATION FOR THE DAY

Our Higher Power does not play games with us. He did not withhold His presence when we needed Him most. He will not refuse to reveal more truths to us, if we continue to be faithful in our search for them. Nor will He withhold the strength we need. Only our selfishness, intellectual pride, fear, greed, and preoccupation with material things can block them out. So long as we are free of such blocks, His spirit will flow into us.

PRAYER FOR THE DAY

I pray that I may never obstruct the flow of life forces I need by preventing God from entering my life. I pray that my faith and trust may remain strong.

JULY 18   THOUGHT FOR THE DAY

Two things can spoil group unity—gossip and criticism. To avoid these divisive things, we must realize that we're all in the same boat. If we're going to be saved, we have to pull together. It is a matter of life or death for us. Gossip and criticism are sure ways of disrupting any group. We're all in the program to keep control of ourselves and to help each other. Neither gossip nor criticism helps anyone maintain rationality. *Am I sometimes guilty of spreading gossip or criticizing?*

MEDITATION FOR THE DAY

Each of us tries to be grateful for the blessings we have received, some of which we do not deserve. Gratitude makes us humble. Before, we did little by ourselves, but now we rely upon a Higher Power to help. No one cares for those who are smug and self-righteous. But nearly everyone is impressed by true humility. Since humility comes from knowing that everything depends upon our relationship to God, we need not worry about losing it, so long as we maintain our faith.

PRAYER FOR THE DAY

I pray that I may walk humbly with God. I pray that I may rely on His grace to carry me through.

Personalities are marvels in their own right. Each of us has one, with its own unique traits. There is no room in this program for gossip. Gossip results from preoccupation with the trivial, the sensational, the trite. It hardly ever has any value or merit. Most often, when problems arise, it is best to discuss them with the person involved, for then one will learn the truth. *Am I careful to avoid gossip about my fellow members?*

MEDITATION FOR THE DAY

To God a miracle of change in a person's life is a natural happening. But it is a natural event operated by spiritual forces. Even though we do not see them as such, miracles happen to those who are fully guided and touched by God. Change often occurs in a person's nature without notice, or it may quickly become apparent to others. Such a miracle usually proceeds from a real desire for change, coupled with the faith that brings it about.

PRAYER FOR THE DAY

I pray that I may expect miracles in the lives of others. I pray that I may be useful in helping others to change.

JULY 20   THOUGHT FOR THE DAY

We must be loyal to the group and to each member of it. We must strive never to accuse members behind their backs or confront them with hostility. It is up to them to tell us if anything is wrong. More than that, we must try not to think hateful things about other members. If we do, we are trying to hurt them. Our group purpose is to be helpful to each other. Cynical distrust is contagious and highly destructive to everyone involved. *Am I a loyal member of and to my group?*

MEDITATION FOR THE DAY

Carry out God's guidance as best you can. Leave the results to Him. Do this obediently and faithfully with no doubt that if the working out of that guidance is left in His hands the results will be all right. Believe that the guidance God gives you has already been worked out by Him to produce the required results for you. God knows your needs, character, and life.

PRAYER FOR THE DAY

I pray that I may live according to the dictates of my conscience. I pray that I may leave the results to God.

If we feel the need to say something to put another member on the right track, we should say it to the person with understanding and compassion, never in a hostile or critical manner. We must keep everything out in the open and completely aboveboard. This is imperative if we are to follow our Twelfth Step way of helping others. Tolerance is vital to group unity, and we all count on it. If we cannot be certain that what we say will be constructive, we should leave it to others who can. *Am I discreet about what I say concerning others and careful to make my comments constructive?*

MEDITATION FOR THE DAY

"Faith can move mountains." That expression means that faith can change any situation in the field of personal relationships. If you trust God, He shows you the way to move mountains. If you are humble enough to know that you can do little by yourself to change a situation, ask God to give you the power you need. Be grateful for His grace, have enough faith, and you can move mountains.

PRAYER FOR THE DAY

I pray that I may have enough faith to make me effective. I pray that I may learn to depend less on myself and more on God.

One of the finest things about this group is the diversity of its membership. We come from all walks and stations of life. All kinds and classes of people are represented in a group. Being different from each other in certain ways, we can each make a different contribution to the whole. Some of us are weak in one respect but strong in another. The group can use the strong points and disregard the others. The group is strong because we all have the same problem and also because we have diverse talents. *Do I recognize the good points of my fellow members?*

MEDITATION FOR THE DAY

"And greater works than these shall ye do." Each individual has the ability to do good works through the power of God's spirit. By gaining experience both in hearing others' troubles and in helping them cope with their situation, we enlarge our capacity to do good. Each of us becomes another emissary of our Higher Power every time we lend a hand to another. Quickly the initial hesitancy is gone. We are not held back by doubt, despondency, or fear. With God's power on which to depend, we have unlimited power to do good.

PRAYER FOR THE DAY

I pray that I may not limit myself by doubts. I pray that I may have confidence that I can be effective for good.

JULY 23   THOUGHT FOR THE DAY

There are no pedestals in our meeting places, nor are there any earthly supreme persons in our membership. A person so singled out is wise to refuse to play such a role. The group is wise not to create such a leader. Without exception we are all only one step away from our old torment, no matter how long we have been in this program. If we insist upon an ideal, it is the program itself, not any one person in it. *Do I put my trust in the principles of my group?*

MEDITATION FOR THE DAY

The inward peace that comes from trust in God truly passes all understanding. That peace no one can take from you. No person has the power to disturb that inner peace. But you must be careful not to let in the world's worries and distractions. You must try not to give entrance to fears and despondency. If you do, you open the door to distractions and eventual disaster. Make it a point today to allow nothing to disturb your inner peace.

PRAYER FOR THE DAY

I pray that I may not allow anyone to spoil my peace of mind. I pray that I may keep an inner calm throughout the day.

Our program is like a dike, holding back the sea of frustrations, uncertainties, fears, uncontrollable emotions. If we permit the smallest hole in the dike, that hole will enlarge to allow an all-consuming flood to drown us. By practicing the principles of this program, we are achieving preventive and corrective maintenance. Our motivation is reasoned: "Instant repair, instant relief." That sea is always there, and we know of its peril from past experience. *Am I ever watchful and mindful of what neglect of the program can cost?*

MEDITATION FOR THE DAY

Keep as close as you can to the Higher Power. Try to think, act, and live as though you were always in God's presence. Keeping close to a Power greater than yourself is the solution to most of the world's problems. Try to practice the presence of God in the things you think and do. This influences the lives of others for good, too. Abide in God and rejoice in His love. Keep God close to your thoughts.

PRAYER FOR THE DAY

I pray that I may keep close to the Mind of God. I pray that I may live with Him in my heart and mind each day.

JULY 25   THOUGHT FOR THE DAY

Many of us are living on borrowed time. We live today because of this program and the grace of God. And for what there is left of our lives we owe to this program and to God. We should make the best use we can of our borrowed time and in some small measure pay back for that part of our lives which we wasted before we came into the program. Our lives from now on are not our own exclusively. We hold them in trust. We must do all we can to forward this great movement which has given us a new lease on life. *Am I aware that I should now be holding my life in trust?*

MEDITATION FOR THE DAY

How much is too much to expect from life? If you hold your life in trust for God, you begin to realize the high value God places on your life. In such an awareness miracles can happen. Life itself becomes a miracle, and the longer you live the more overwhelming is the proof that many good things are in store for you. God is Lord of your life, Controller of your days, and Governor of your future.

PRAYER FOR THE DAY

I pray that I may hold my life in trust for God. I pray that I may no longer consider it mine alone.

When we come to the end of our lives, we will take no material thing with us. We will not take one cent in our cold, dead hands. The only things that we take are the things we have given away. If we have helped others, we may take that with us. If we have given of our time and money for the good of this program, we may take that with us. Looking back over our lives, what are we proud of? Not what we have gained for ourselves, but what good we have done. *What will I take with me when I go?*

MEDITATION FOR THE DAY

"Hallowed be Thy Name." What does that mean to us? Here *name* is used in the sense of "spirit." The words mean praise to God for His spirit in the world, making us better. We should be especially grateful for God's spirit, which gives us the strength to overcome all that is base in our lives. His spirit is powerful. It can help us live a conquering, abundant life. We praise and thank Him for His spirit in our lives.

PRAYER FOR THE DAY

I pray that I may be grateful for God's spirit in me. I pray that I may try to live in accordance with it.

JULY 27 THOUGHT FOR THE DAY

To paraphrase the Psalm: "We victims of turmoil de-
clare the power of distress, and torment showeth its
handiwork. Day unto day uttereth crises, and night
unto night showeth our suffering. The law of our
program is perfect, converting the irrational. The testimony of our meetings is sure, making wise the simple. The steps of our program are right, rejoicing the
heart. The procedure of our meeting is pure, en-
lightening the members. The fear of a step backward
is intense, enduring forever." *Have I any doubt about
the power of returned misery through distress?*

MEDITATION FOR THE DAY

Walking with God means practicing the presence of
God in your daily affairs. It means asking Him for
strength to face each new day. It means turning to
Him often during the day in meditation, for yourself
and for others. Nothing can seriously upset you if
you remember Him. He is beside you in spirit, to help
and guide you.

PRAYER FOR THE DAY

I pray that I may try to walk with God. I pray that I
may turn to Him often as to a close friend.

To continue the paraphrase of the Psalm: "The judgments of the twelve steps are true and righteous altogether. More to be desired are they than any excess of living, sweeter also than turmoil. Moreover, by them are members warned, and in following them there is great reward. Who can understand our affliction? Cleanse us from secret faults. Keep us from presumptuous resentments. Let them not have dominion over us. Then shall we be upright and free of the great transgression." *Am I resolved that affliction will never again have dominion over me?*

MEDITATION FOR THE DAY

God can be your shield. Then no buffets of the world can harm you. Between you and all scorn and indignity from others is your trust in God, like a shining shield. Nothing can then have the power to spoil your inward peace. With this shield you can attain inward peace quickly, in your surroundings as well as in your heart. You need not resent the person who troubles you but can overcome the resentment.

PRAYER FOR THE DAY

I pray that I may strive for inward peace. I pray that I may not be seriously upset, no matter what happens.

JULY 29   THOUGHT FOR THE DAY

There are two days in every week about which we should not worry. These two days should be kept from regret and fear. One of these days is yesterday, with its mistakes and cares, its faults and blunders, its aches and pains. Yesterday has passed forever beyond our control. All the money in the world cannot bring back yesterday. We cannot undo a single act we performed. We cannot erase a single word we said. Yesterday is gone beyond recall. *Do I still worry about what happened yesterday?*

MEDITATION FOR THE DAY

If you have enough faith, God will give you all the strength you need to face every temptation and overcome it. Nothing will prove too hard for you to bear. You can face any situation. So fear nothing. "Every temptation?" you ask, and again, "Any situation?" Yes, if you have enough faith.

PRAYER FOR THE DAY

I pray that I may have strength to overcome every temptation. I pray that I may have enough faith to face any situation.

The other day about which we should not worry is tomorrow, with its possible adversities, its burdens, its large promise, and perhaps its poor performance. Tomorrow is also beyond our immediate control. Tomorrow's sun will rise, either in splendor or behind a mask of clouds, but it will rise. Until it does, we have no stake in tomorrow, for it is as yet unborn. *Do I still worry too much about tomorrow?*

MEDITATION FOR THE DAY

"Faith is the substance of things hoped for, the evidence of things not seen." Faith is not seeing but believing. Down through the ages there have always been those who obeyed the heavenly vision, not seeing but believing in God. And their faith was rewarded. You cannot see God, but you can see the results of faith in human lives, changing them from defeat to victory.

PRAYER FOR THE DAY

I pray that I may have faith enough to believe without seeing. I pray that I may be content with the results of my faith.

There is one more day to consider—today. Anyone can fight the battles of just one day. It is only when you and I add the burden of those two awful eternities, yesterday and tomorrow, that we break down. It is not the experience of today that drives us mad. It is the remorse or bitterness for something that happened yesterday or the dread of what tomorrow may bring. Let us therefore do our best to live but one day at a time. *Am I living one day at a time?*

MEDITATION FOR THE DAY

Give your Higher Power the gift of a thankful heart. Try to see causes for thankfulness in your everyday life. When life seems hard and troubles crowd in, then look for some reasons for thankfulness. There is nearly always something you can be thankful for. The offering of thanksgiving is indeed a sweet incense going up to God throughout a busy day. You will acquire in time the habit of being constantly grateful to God for all His blessings. Each new day some new cause for joy will spring to your mind.

PRAYER FOR THE DAY

I pray for a truly thankful heart. I pray that I may be constantly reminded of reasons for sincere gratitude.

AUGUST 1   THOUGHT FOR THE DAY

This program has borrowed from medicine, psychiatry, and religion. It has taken from these what it wanted and combined it into the program that it considers is best suited to the members' needs and will best help them recover. The results have been very satisfactory. We do not try to improve on this program. Its value has been proved by the success it has had in helping many thousands to recover. It has everything we need to arrest our affliction. *Do I try to follow the program just as it is?*

MEDITATION FOR THE DAY

You should strive for a union between your purposes in life and the purposes of the Divine Principle directing the universe. There is no bond of union on earth to compare with the union between a human soul and God. Priceless beyond all earth's rewards is that union. In merging your heart and mind with the Higher Power, you experience a oneness of purpose that puts you in harmony with God and all others who are trying to do His will.

PRAYER FOR THE DAY

I pray that I may become attuned to the will of God. I pray that I may be in harmony with the music of the universe.

AUGUST 2   THOUGHT FOR THE DAY

This program has no quarrel with medicine, psychiatry, or religion. We have great respect for the methods of each. And we are glad for any success they may have had with any of us. We are desirous always of cooperating with them in every way. The more doctors, the more psychiatrists, the more clergymen and rabbis we can get to work with us, the better we like it. We have many who take a real interest in our program, and we would like many more. *Am I ready to cooperate with those who take a sincere interest in this program?*

MEDITATION FOR THE DAY

God is always ready to pour His blessings into our hearts in generous measure. But like the seed-sowing, the ground must be prepared before the seed is dropped in. It is our task to prepare the soil. It is God's role to drop in the seed. This preparation of the soil means many days of right living, choosing the right way and avoiding the wrong. As you go along, each day you are better prepared for God's planting, until you reach the time of harvest. Then you share the harvest with God—the harvest of a useful and abundant life.

PRAYER FOR THE DAY

I pray that my way of living may be properly prepared day by day. I pray that I may strive to make myself ready for the harvest that God has planted in my heart.

AUGUST 3   THOUGHT FOR THE DAY

In this program we are offering something intangible. We are offering a psychological and spiritual program. We are not offering a medical program. If someone needs medical treatment, we call in a doctor. If someone needs a medical prescription, we let the doctor prescribe for him. If someone needs hospital treatment, we let the hospital take care of him. Our vital work begins when the person is physically able to receive it. *Am I willing to leave medical care to the doctors?*

MEDITATION FOR THE DAY

Each moment of your day that you devote to this new way of life is a gift of God. The gift of the moments, even when you desire to serve God, is not an easy thing to give. The things you had planned to do, given up gladly so that you can perform a service, are your eventual reward, not a sacrifice. Every situation has two interpretations, your own and God's. Try to handle each situation in the way you believe God would wish it handled.

PRAYER FOR THE DAY

I pray that I may make my day count somewhat for God. I pray that I may not spend it all selfishly.

AUGUST 4   THOUGHT FOR THE DAY

We are offering a kind of psychological program as well as a spiritual one. First, people must be mentally able to receive it. They must be convinced that they want rationality and be willing to do something about it. Their confidence must be obtained. We must show them that we are true friends and really desire to help. When we have their confidence, they will listen to us. The fellowship is a kind of group therapy. Newcomers need the fellowship of others who understand their affliction because they have it themselves. They must learn to re-educate their minds. They must learn to think differently, become willing to see fears, faults, failures. *Do I do my best to give this mental help?*

MEDITATION FOR THE DAY

"And this is life eternal, that they may know Thee." It is the flow of the life eternal through spirit, mind, and body that cleanses, heals, restores, and renews. Seek conscious contact with God more and more each day. Make God an abiding presence during the day. Be conscious of His spirit helping you. All that is done without God's spirit is merely passing. All that is done with His spirit is life eternal.

PRAYER FOR THE DAY

I pray that I may be in the stream of eternal life. I pray that I may be cleansed and healed by the Eternal Spirit.

AUGUST 5 THOUGHT FOR THE DAY

We are offering a spiritual program. The basis of this fellowship is belief in a Power greater than ourselves. This belief takes us off the center of the universe and allows us to transfer our problems to a Power outside ourselves. We turn to this Power for the strength we need to regain rationality and to stay sensible. We put our problems in the hands of God and leave them there. We stop trying to run our own lives and let God run them for us. *Do I do my best to give spiritual help?*

MEDITATION FOR THE DAY

God is your healer and your strength. You do not have to ask Him to come to you. He is always with you in spirit. Your need is God's opportunity. You must learn to rely on His strength whenever you need it. To indulge feelings of inadequacy is to be disloyal to God. Just say to yourself, "I know that He is with me and will help me."

PRAYER FOR THE DAY

I pray that I may never feel inadequate to any situation. I pray that I may be buoyed up by the feeling that God is with me.

AUGUST 6 THOUGHT FOR THE DAY

Psychologists are turning to religion because just knowing about ourselves is not enough. We need the added dynamic of faith in a Power greater than ourselves on which we can rely. Books on psychology and psychiatric treatment are not enough, without the strength that comes from faith in God. And clergymen and rabbis have turned to psychology because faith is an act of the mind and will. Religion must be presented in psychological terms to some extent in order to satisfy the modern man. Faith must be built largely on our own psychological experience. *Have I taken what I need from both psychology and religion when I live this program?*

MEDITATION FOR THE DAY

Refilling with the spirit is something you need every day. For this refilling with the spirit you need these times of quiet meditation away, alone, without noise, without activity. From these times of communion you come forth with new power. This refilling is the best preparation for effective work.

PRAYER FOR THE DAY

I pray that I may be daily refilled with the right spirit. I pray that I may be full of the joy of true living.

In this program we are offering an intangible thing, a psychological and spiritual program. It's a wonderful program. We learn to turn to a Higher Power. With faith in that Higher Power we are given the strength we need and peace of mind. We re-educate our minds by learning to think differently, to find new interests that make our lives worthwhile. We who have achieved rationality through faith in God and mental re-education are modern miracles. It is the function of our program to produce modern miracles. *Do I consider the change in my life a modern miracle?*

MEDITATION FOR THE DAY

You should never doubt that God's spirit is always with you, wherever you are, to keep you on the right path. God's keeping power is never absent, only your realization of it. Not His shelter but whether or not you seek its security is the question. Every fear, worry, or doubt is a kind of disloyalty to God. You must endeavor to trust Him wholly. Assure yourself that all is going to be well. Say it to yourself until you feel it deeply.

PRAYER FOR THE DAY

I pray that I may feel deeply that all is well. I pray that nothing will be able to move me from that deep conviction.

AUGUST 8   THOUGHT FOR THE DAY

For a while we are going back to the philosophy of our program, so that we may fix segments of it in our minds. There is no substitute for this basic philosophy. It is our way of faith, our "bible." We should study it thoroughly and make it a part of ourselves. We should not try to change any of it. Within its steps is the full exposition of the program. There is no easy, effortless alternative. We should examine it often. *Have I studied the program's philosophy faithfully?*

MEDITATION FOR THE DAY

All of life is a fluctuation between effort and rest. You need both every day. But effort is not truly effective until first you have had the proper preparation for it, by resting in a time of quiet meditation. This daily time of rest gives you the power necessary to make your best effort. There are days when you expend much effort, and there are times when you need rest. The successful life is a proper balance between the two.

PRAYER FOR THE DAY

I pray that I may be ready to make the proper effort. I pray that I may also recognize the need for relaxation.

AUGUST 9 THOUGHT FOR THE DAY

We have a susceptibility to a certain affliction. Particular attitudes or events produce in us a manifestation of this affliction. As vulnerable people we can never safely indulge in certain behavior or its causes. Unless we can experience a psychological change in attitude, our lives will be filled with turmoil and suffering. Once we are changed, we who seemed doomed find ourselves able to control our susceptibility. *Have I had this change of attitude?*

MEDITATION FOR THE DAY

At first we all doubt that we have the strength to change. If we had moments when our affliction recurred, we came away more convinced that there was no real hope. The rescue from this deep state of despair sometimes shocks us. We hear the phrase "reaching bottom" and know how it feels. In all instances a renewal of faith is imperative to recovery, and we call upon a Higher Power for help. Our continuance thereafter, free of that misery, almost always depends upon our continuance of contact with our Higher Power.

PRAYER FOR THE DAY

I pray that I may be daily willing to be changed. I pray that I may put myself wholly in God's hands for the continuance of my recovery.

AUGUST 10   THOUGHT FOR THE DAY

The really startling revelation for every one of us in this program is that we have discovered a common solution. We who have found this solution to our problem and are armed with facts about ourselves can win others' confidence. We are able to approach others knowing that we've been there. Our whole manner tells them that we are the ones with the answer they need. *Am I a person with a real answer to another's distress?*

MEDITATION FOR THE DAY

There are benefits for the person who is recovering, but there are still responsibilities. While we hear it said that things can only get better or that good things start to happen, this does not mean that no more reversals in life will come. By considering that we still live essentially a normal life, we recall that it is normal to have heartache, trials, failures, and dismay. One of the things we will use to overcome these is our faith in a Higher Power. Perhaps we had never practiced any real dependence on this before. Now we realize how comforting it is.

PRAYER FOR THE DAY

I pray that I may keep my feet on the way. I pray that I may make continuous efforts to seek God's comfort in time of need.

While each of us stays strictly clear of our affliction, we react to life much like other persons. The first recurrence of that misery would set the terrible cycle in motion again. Sufferers usually have no true idea why they allow this to happen. Some have excuses with which they are satisfied, but in their hearts they really do not know why it happened. The truth is that at some point down the way they passed the point where the most powerful desire to stop was of no avail. *Am I satisfied that I can never allow a recurrence of my affliction?*

MEDITATION FOR THE DAY

Out of the darkness He is leading you to light. Out of unrest to rest, out of disorder to order, out of faults and failures God leads to success. He can bring peace and order out of your private chaos if you will let Him. In the time you have been with this group, you have been witness to some of His handiwork. That it has no limit is clear to us all.

PRAYER FOR THE DAY

I pray that I may be led out of disorder into order. I pray that I may be ever mindful of how my life might have been and how I have been led to light.

There is virtually no way left but for us to pick up the simple spiritual tools laid at our feet by this program. In so doing, we have a spiritual experience that revolutionizes our whole attitude toward life. Since our affliction developed partly as a result of our lack of faith, too little trust, being without real love, we can readily understand how turning our situation over to a Higher Power is our acknowledgment that we need them in our struggle to recover. *Will I continue to go the way this program leads me?*

MEDITATION FOR THE DAY

The moment a thing seems wrong to you or a person's actions seem to be other than what you think they should be, at that moment you begin your obligation to pray that the thing be righted or the person changed. It is not your responsibility to interfere or take control, but your prayers and your behavior can have influence for good. You may see lives altered and evils banished.

PRAYER FOR THE DAY

I pray that I may be a co-worker with God. I pray that I may help people by my example.

We had but two alternatives. One was to go on to the disastrous end, totally repressing the awareness of our intolerable situation. The other was to accept our plight and seek a spiritual solution. We became willing to maintain a certain simple attitude toward life. What seemed at first a flimsy reed has proved to be the loving and powerful hand of God. A new life has been given to us. Each of us molds in his own way his personal solutions to his problems. *Have I evolved a workable attitude toward my situation?*

MEDITATION FOR THE DAY

Make it a daily practice to review your character. Review it in relation to your daily life, your loved ones, your friends, and your work. Each day try to see where God wants you to change. Plan how best each fault can be eliminated, each mistake corrected. Comparisons to others will not work. Strive for a better life as your ultimate goal.

PRAYER FOR THE DAY

I pray that I may make real progress toward a better life. I pray that I may never be satisfied with my present state.

AUGUST 14   THOUGHT FOR THE DAY

No person likes to think that he is physically and mentally different from others. Our afflictions have been characterized by countless vain attempts to prove that we could restrain our turmoil as others handle their problems. This delusion that we are like other people has to be shattered. It has been definitely proved that none of us has ever recovered a normal person's limits of control. Over any considerable period we get worse, never better. *Am I convinced that I will never be like normal persons about my distress again?*

MEDITATION FOR THE DAY

There are times when we need to show great patience. We had no trouble summoning the energies we needed to indulge our distress. We now recognize that each of us has the capacity to develop patience. This virtue can be learned, but it is also given to us through meditation and prayer. Though we sometimes do not know how we learn to have patience, it is enough for now to know that we can learn. Meditation can help answer many of our questions, and it affords the training ground to learn to have patience.

PRAYER FOR THE DAY

I pray that I may accept the gift of an abundant spiritual life. I pray that my patience will grow with each new day.

AUGUST 15   THOUGHT FOR THE DAY

Reverting to the old turmoil after a period of recovery soon puts us in a situation as bad as or worse than before. If we have admitted that we are vulnerable, we must have no reservations of any kind, or any lurking notion that someday we will be able to experiment again. What sort of thinking dominates anyone who repeats time after time the desperate experiment of that irrationality? Parallel with sound reasoning there inevitably runs some wholly bizarre excuse for taking the step backward to disaster. *Have I given up all excuses for indulging such madness again?*

MEDITATION FOR THE DAY

The grace of God can come to people who are together in one place with one accord. A union like this is miracle-working. God is able to use such people. Only good can come through such an experience, and this is the atmosphere that prevails in our group meetings. We are brought together in unified groups for a single purpose and of a single mind. That we profit immeasurably is no accident.

PRAYER FOR THE DAY

I pray that I may continue to be a part of a unified group. I pray that I may contribute my share to its consecrated purposes.

An afflicted person is absolutely unable to prevent personal chaos on the basis of self-knowledge. We must admit that we can do nothing about it ourselves. Will power and self-knowledge will never help in the strange mental blank spots when we are tempted to revert to turmoil. In these throes the victim is in a hopeless condition. The last flicker of conviction that we can do the job ourselves must be snuffed out. We are completely helpless apart from divine help. The spiritual answer is the only true hope. *Have I accepted the spiritual answer as the answer I've sought?*

MEDITATION FOR THE DAY

Frustration is another challenge that can well be unbearable torment. In moments like that one is essentially without defense, for reason wanes, and pressure for relief mounts. Since the elements of frustration are within our minds, we have an option to use our minds to counteract them. We remember all the things this program has taught us. First and foremost is our dependence upon our Higher Power to guide us, afford release, and quell the anguish. Though it is difficult at first, we meditate and grow until frustration becomes almost nonexistent in our lives.

PRAYER FOR THE DAY

I pray that the peace I have found will make me effective. I pray that I may be relieved of frustration during the day.

To one who feels he is an atheist or agnostic, a spiritual experience seems unlikely or impossible; but to continue as he is means disaster. To be doomed to a living death or to live on a spiritual basis are not always easy alternatives. But we have to face the fact that we must find a spiritual basis of life or meet disaster. Lack of power is our dilemma. We have to find a power by which we can live, and it has to be a Power greater than ourselves. *Have I found that Power by which I can now live?*

MEDITATION FOR THE DAY

Sunshine is the laughter of nature. Live in the sun. The sun and air are good medicine. Nature is a good nurse for tired bodies. Let her have her way with you. God's grace is like the sunshine. Let your whole being be wrapped in the Divine Spirit. Faith is the soul's breathing in of the Divine Spirit. Let the Divine Spirit have its way, and all will be well.

PRAYER FOR THE DAY

I pray that I may live in the sunshine of God's spirit. I pray that my mind and soul may be wrapped in it.

The agnostics among us have recognized that once they were able to dismiss their prejudices and express a belief in a Power greater than themselves they commenced to get results. They found that it was impossible to define or comprehend that Power which we call God. As soon as they can say that they believe or are willing to believe, they are on the way. *Am I willing to depend on a Power that I cannot fully define or comprehend?*

MEDITATION FOR THE DAY

We seek God's presence, and it is not a question of searching so much as an inner consciousness of His presence. To realize God's presence, you must surrender in the small things in life as well as the big things. This makes His guidance possible. Some things put a distance between your mind and God, such as a fear-inspired failure, a harsh criticism, a stubborn resentment. We are brought closer by a word of love, a selfless reconciliation, a kind act of helpfulness.

PRAYER FOR THE DAY

I pray that I may think and say and do the things that bring God closer to me. I pray that I may find Him in a word of love or an unselfish deed.

Those who have faith have a sound, rational idea of what life is all about. There is considerable difference in how each of us conceives of the Power greater than ourselves. It is not at all important whether or not we agree with each other about this. We have questions that we must resolve ourselves. But in every one of our situations the belief in a Higher Power has been what accomplished the miraculous, the humanly impossible. We have lived a revolutionary change in our existence and in our thinking. *Has there been a revolutionary change in me?*

MEDITATION FOR THE DAY

Worship is consciousness of God's divine majesty. As you pause to worship, God will help you raise your humanity to His divinity. The earth is a material temple to enclose God's divinity. God brings to those who worship Him a divine power, a divine love, and a divine healing. You have only to open your mind to Him and try to absorb some of His divine spirit. Pausing quietly in the spirit of worship, turn your inward thoughts upward and realize that His divine power may be yours, that you can experience His love and healing.

PRAYER FOR THE DAY

I pray that I may worship God by sensing the eternal Spirit. I pray that I may experience a new power in my life.

AUGUST 20 THOUGHT FOR THE DAY

You should not dwell too much on the mistakes, faults, and failures of the past. Be done with shame and remorse. Abandon contempt for yourself and develop a new self-respect. Unless you do this, others will not respect you. The race is run, and you did not win but stumbled and fell. You have risen once again and now are on the way to the goal of a better life. Do not stay to examine the place where it all happened. Regret only the delay and your lack of vision about the real goals. Many others have been in your position before, and there will be more to come. *Do I realize that life is not over because I lost one contest?*

MEDITATION FOR THE DAY

Many people have said that the awareness of the presence of God is the most important fact of their lives. This is a compelling reason for one to have faith. We stop doubting the power of God when we see others solve their problems by simple reliance on a Higher Power. Ideas alone do not work. Faith in a Power greater than ourselves allows all things to occur. Here, during this moment today, I have an awareness of that Power, the influence it can have on my life, and the inherent promise that it will be present again tomorrow, if I but ask for it.

PRAYER FOR THE DAY

I pray that I may be conscious of God's presence as the most compelling event in my life. I pray that each day may begin and end with His blessing.

This is a physical, mental, and spiritual program. Who are we to say that there is no Higher Power? This challenge comes to us all. Can we deny that there is a design and purpose in life? Or are we willing to admit that faith in some Divine Principle is a vital part of our lives, just as is our love for other persons? We can find truth deep within us if we confront ourselves as we are. Some of us do not find a Higher Power, and others deny that one exists. In the final search, it is only deep down within us that our Higher Power may be found. *Do I understand that faith means accepting what I cannot know by reason?*

MEDITATION FOR THE DAY

"Behold, I make all things new." When you change to a new way of life, you leave many things behind you. Loosen some of the strands so that the earthbound spirit can soar. Earthly desires bind, but your new freedom gives you the ability to rise above these. Injuries will mend, as will broken lives. The Healer assures us that He will restore us. Spiritual mending is imperative to us all. Wonder not that it happens, but give thanks to God that it has.

PRAYER FOR THE DAY

I pray that I may be freed from hesitancy and doubt. I pray that I may continue to praise God for my new way of life.

From A.A. we quote: "Those who do not recover are people who are constitutionally incapable of being honest with themselves. There are such unfortunates. They are not at fault. They seem to be born that way." Alcoholics are not the only persons like that. The message clearly refers to many others. "They are naturally incapable of grasping and developing a manner of living which demands rigorous honesty. Their chances are less than average. There are those too who suffer from grave emotional and mental disorders, but many of them do recover, if they have the capacity to be honest." Here it is, stated as well as we could ask. Personal honesty counts very heavily in any recovery, but it is absolutely required in this program. *Am I honest with myself and others?*

MEDITATION FOR THE DAY

You can make use of your mistakes, failures, losses, and suffering. It is not what happens to you but what you make of it. The program demands that you give away what you have received. Then something good comes of your suffering. The world will improve because of it. The distress and pain will pass. All this transpires through the Divine Spirit's intervention on your behalf. You cannot do it alone.

PRAYER FOR THE DAY

I pray that I may profit from mistakes and failures. I pray that some good may result from my agonies.

AUGUST 23   THOUGHT FOR THE DAY

When we accepted our program's principles, we were faced with the necessity for a thorough personal housecleaning. We faced and rid ourselves of the things that blocked us. Now we continue to take a personal inventory, to take stock honestly. We search out flaws that caused failures. Resentment heads the list. Futility and unhappiness are the only outcome if life includes deep resentment. *Am I free of resentment and anger?*

MEDITATION FOR THE DAY

Keep in mind the goal you are striving for, the good life you are trying to attain. Do not let little things divert you from the path. Do not be overcome by the small trials and vexations of each day. Try to see the purpose and plan to which all is leading. If when climbing a mountain you keep your eyes on each stony or difficult place, how weary is your climb. Think of the summit, and each step is worthwhile. Each problem you encounter may be God's test of your willingness to persist.

PRAYER FOR THE DAY

I pray that I may realize that life without a goal is futile. I pray that I may find the good life worth striving for.

When we recognized our faults, we made a list of them. We wrote them down. We admitted our wrongs openly and honestly and resolved to set them right. We recognized our fears and asked God to remove them. Many of us realized that we had an unhealthy attitude about sex. We came to understand how these God-given capacities were good only if used properly, never selfishly or lightly and never despised or resented. If sex was troublesome to us, we threw ourselves the harder into helping others. *Am I facing my problems about sex in the proper way?*

MEDITATION FOR THE DAY

Cling to the belief that all things are possible with a Higher Power. If you truly accept this belief, it is the ladder upon which a human soul can climb from the lowest pit of despair to the greatest heights. It is possible for God to change your way of living. When you see the change in another through the grace of God, you cannot doubt. All things are possible through faith.

PRAYER FOR THE DAY

I pray that I may live expectantly. I pray that I may believe deeply that all things are possible with God.

This program urges us to discuss our defects with another person. This is an acid test. If we fail to do this, we will not acquire enough humility, fearlessness, or honesty to really get the program. We must be honest if we hope to live happily. We must be hard on ourselves and yet considerate of others. We swallow our pride and plunge into that darkness of the past, illuminating each character warp, each hidden recess. Once we take this step, withholding nothing, we can face the world squarely. *Have I discussed all my defects with another person?*

MEDITATION FOR THE DAY

Never yield to weariness of the spirit. At times the world's cares and distractions will intrude, and the spirit will become weak. At times like this carry on, and soon the spirit will become strong again. None ever sincerely sought God's help in vain. Exhaustion and weariness make a time of communion with a Higher Power vital. When you are inundated by temporary adversities, keep quiet and wait for His spirit to flow back.

PRAYER FOR THE DAY

I pray that I may not speak or act in the midst of emotional unrest and confusion. I pray that I may wait until the tempest is passed.

While we may readily give up most of ourselves, we may cling to something that we will not give up. We must ask the Higher Power to help us become willing to let even that go too. We can't compartmentalize our lives, keeping some for ourselves. We must give it all to Him. We must yield to God the good, the bad, and the undefined. We then implore Him to remove every single defect that stands in the way of our usefulness. *Am I still clinging to something that I will not let go?*

MEDITATION FOR THE DAY

The laws of nature cannot be changed. They must be obeyed if you are to stay healthy. No exceptions will be made in your case. Submit to the laws of nature, or they will finally break you. In the realm of the spirit, in all human relationships, submit to the moral laws and to the will of God. If you continue to break the laws of honesty, purity, unselfishness, and love, you will be broken to some extent yourself. The moral and spiritual laws of God, like the laws of nature, are unbreakable without some disaster.

PRAYER FOR THE DAY

I pray that I may submit to the laws of nature and to the laws of God. I pray that I may live in harmony with all the laws of life.

Again from A.A.: "We must be willing to make amends to all the people we have harmed. We must do the best we can to repair the damage done in the past." When we make amends, the other person is sure to recognize our sincere desire to right the wrong. Others may even admit their own fault, and feuds of long standing are dissolved. Iron-fisted creditors will sometimes amaze us. In general, we must be willing to put things right, no matter the consequences to us. *Have I made a sincere effort to make amends to the people I have harmed?*

MEDITATION FOR THE DAY

The grace of God cures disharmony and disorder in human relationships. Directly you put your affairs, with their confusion and their difficulties, into His hands, He begins to effect a cure of all that chaos. You can believe that He will cause you no more pain in the doing of it than would a physician who knows what he can do to cure you. Have faith that your Higher Power will do all that is necessary as painlessly as possible. But you must be willing to submit to His treatment, even if you cannot now see the meaning or purpose of it.

PRAYER FOR THE DAY

I pray that I may willingly submit to whatever spiritual discipline is necessary. I pray that I may accept whatever it takes to live a better life.

AUGUST 28   THOUGHT FOR THE DAY

Our personal inventory is a continuing thing, to set right any new mistakes we make each day. Our responsibility is to mature in effective understanding. We cannot expect to achieve this overnight, but as a continuum for life. We must be ever watchful for selfishness, resentment, fear, and dishonesty. When any of these arise, we seek our Higher Power's help at once to overcome them. There is no reprieve, no vacation, no respite from the task. We are not cured, but have only a daily reprieve, contingent upon continuing our spiritual condition. *Am I checking my spiritual condition daily?*

MEDITATION FOR THE DAY

Happiness cannot be sought directly; it is a by-product of love and service. Service is a law of our being. With love in your heart, there is always some service to others that yields to you a life of power and joy and satisfaction. Persons who hate or are selfish are going against the laws of their own beings. They are cut off from God and others. Little acts of love and encouragement, of service and help erase the rough places of life and help make the path smooth. Thus we gain our share of happiness.

PRAYER FOR THE DAY

I pray that I may give my share of love and service. I pray that I may not grow weary in my attempts to do the right thing.

AUGUST 29   THOUGHT FOR THE DAY

Since this is a spiritual program, in addition to its
other aspects, we rely on prayer and meditation. Each
day we start our twenty-four hours by considering
our plans. Before we begin, we ask our Higher Power
to direct our thinking, to elevate our thoughts. We
conclude our meditation by asking that we will be
shown through the day what our next step is to be.
We cannot do all this as mere ritual, for it becomes
meaningless. We cannot entertain any reservation,
for that is hypocritical. *Am I sincere in my desire to do
God's will today?*

MEDITATION FOR THE DAY

Breathe in the inspiration of goodness and truth. It is
the spirit of honesty, purity, unselfishness, and love.
It is readily available if we are willing to accept it
wholeheartedly. God has given us two things—His
spirit and the power of choice. We can accept them or
not, as we will. We have the gift of a free will. If we
choose selfishness and pride, we reject His spirit.
When we choose the path of love and service, we
accept God's spirit, and it flows into us and makes all
things new.

PRAYER FOR THE DAY

I pray that I may choose the right way. I pray that I
may follow it to the end.

A practical lesson learned from this program is that immunity from our afflictions is assured when we are doing extensive work with others like us. Carry the message to others. You can help when no one else can. You can gain their confidence when others fail. Life acquires a new meaning for you. To watch the recovery of others, to see it passed on by them, to banish loneliness, to see your group grow, to gain new friends—you must not miss such experiences. *Am I always ready and willing to help others?*

MEDITATION FOR THE DAY

One secret of abundant living is the art of giving. The paradox of life is that the more you give the more you have. If you lose your life in the service of others, you will save it. You can give abundantly and so live abundantly. You are rich in one respect—you have a spirit that is inexhaustible. Give your personal ease and comfort, your time, your money, and, most of all, yourself.

PRAYER FOR THE DAY

I pray that I may live to give. I pray that I may learn this secret of abundant living.

Make your first contact with new prospects while they are somewhat down. They may be more receptive when they are depressed. See them alone, if possible, and tell enough about your own encounters, symptoms, and experiences to encourage them to talk as well. If they wish to talk, fine. If not, tell about the troubles your turmoil has caused you, but do not moralize or lecture. When they see that you know the true picture, then begin to describe yourself as a distressed person and tell how you learned that you were so. *Am I ready to talk about myself to prospects?*

MEDITATION FOR THE DAY

Try not to give way to criticism, blame, scorn, or judgment when you are trying to help another. Twelfth Step effectiveness depends on controlling yourself. You may be naturally inclined to blame, but keep a tight rein on your emotions. Be the motive to seek the program, not the cause for further chaos. You need a firm foundation of spiritual living that makes you truly humble, if you are to help others. Be easy on them—tolerance—and hard on yourself—restraint. That is the way you can be used most to uplift a despairing spirit.

PRAYER FOR THE DAY

I pray that I may try to avoid judgment and criticism. I pray that I may always try to build up a person, not tear him down.

SEPTEMBER 1   THOUGHT FOR THE DAY

As you talk to new prospects, be cautious not to brand them as afflicted. Let them draw their own conclusion. But do talk about the hopelessness of the affliction. Tell them exactly what happened to you, how you recovered. Stress the spiritual feature freely. If they are agnostics or atheists, make it emphatic that the Higher Power is one as we understand Him. They can choose any conception they like provided it makes sense to them. They face no awesome force, but a Power greater than themselves, and they are asked to live by principles in keeping with this. *Do I hold back too much in speaking of the spiritual principles of this program?*

MEDITATION FOR THE DAY

Down through the centuries thousands have believed in God's constancy, untiringness, and unfailing love. You are assured of His love. In every difficulty and temptation you are assured of His strength. Always there is One who is patient; always there is One who understands and whom you will understand. You will never be left alone.

PRAYER FOR THE DAY

I pray that I may feel that God's love will never fail. I pray that I may have confidence in His unfailing power.

SEPTEMBER 2   THOUGHT FOR THE DAY

The new prospects want to know how the program works. Explain how you appraised yourself, how you straightened out your past, why you are now trying to help them. It is imperative that they realize that your attempt to pass it on to them is a vital part of your own recovery. The more hopeless they feel the better just now. They will be more likely to follow your suggestions. Tell them about the fellowship of the group and that we share the same affliction. *Can I explain this program to another sufferer?*

MEDITATION FOR THE DAY

You should try to stand aside and let the Higher Power work through you. You should try not to block Him off by your own efforts or prevent His spirit working through you. God desires your obedient service and your loyalty to the ideals of the new life you are seeking. If you are loyal to the Higher Power, He will give you protection against mistakes. Real success will come if you put yourself in the background and let Him work through you.

PRAYER FOR THE DAY

I pray that I may not interfere with the working of the Spirit in me. I pray that it may be given full rein.

SEPTEMBER 3   THOUGHT FOR THE DAY

New prospects need your offer of friendship and fellowship. Tell them that you will do whatever you can to help them recover, and reinforce the belief that they can get well, regardless of anyone else. Job or no job, married or not, they cannot recover from their affliction as long as they depend on others instead of on their Higher Power. Some will argue they cannot recover unless they have their families back. This is false. Their recovery does not depend on others. It depends upon their relationship to their Higher Power. *Do I encourage prospects to depend on their Higher Power?*

MEDITATION FOR THE DAY

The spiritual life depends upon the Unseen. To live the spiritual life, you must believe in the Unseen. Try not to lose the consciousness of God's spirit in you and in others. As a child in its mother's arms, stay sheltered in the understanding and love of God. The Higher Power will relieve you of the worry, the maddening craving, the physical torment, the misery, the depression, the feeling of hopelessness, the hateful anger, the utter confusion. Lift up your eyes from earth's troubles, and you will see.

PRAYER FOR THE DAY

I pray that I may rest and abide in the presence of the unseen God. I pray that I may leave my burdens in His care.

SEPTEMBER 4   THOUGHT FOR THE DAY

As "spokesmen" for this program, we should never show intolerance or hatred of those with afflictions. Experience shows that such an attitude is not helpful to anyone. We are not intolerant of those who can indulge safely in what we must avoid. Prospects would not feel at ease with us if they felt we were fanatics. Temperate indulgence is all right for others. We can't afford the risk, but we shall be of little use if our attitude is one of bitterness and hostility. *Do I have tolerance for those who can indulge safely in what I must avoid?*

MEDITATION FOR THE DAY

Do not become encumbered by petty annoyances. Never respond to emotional upset by more emotional upset. Try to keep calm in all circumstances. Try not to fight back. Call on the grace of God to calm you when you feel like retaliating. Look to God for the inner strength to drop those resentments that drag you down. If you are burdened by annoyances, you will lose your inward peace, and the spirit of God will be shut out. Try to stay serene within.

PRAYER FOR THE DAY

I pray that I may do the things that make for peace. I pray that I may have a mission of conciliation.

SEPTEMBER 5   THOUGHT FOR THE DAY

One of the mottoes of our program is "First Things First." This means that we should always keep in mind that excessiveness is our number one problem. We must never let any other problem, whether of family, business, friends, or anything else, take precedence in our minds over our need to overcome our afflictions. As we go along in this program, we learn to recognize the things that may upset us. When we find ourselves getting upset over something, we must realize that it's a luxury we can't afford. Anything that makes us forget our number one problem is dangerous to us. *Am I keeping my goal of overcoming my affliction in first place in my mind?*

MEDITATION FOR THE DAY

Spiritual progress is the law of your being. Try to see around you more and more of beauty and truth, knowledge and power. Today try to be stronger, braver, more loving as a result of what you did yesterday. This law of spiritual progress gives meaning and purpose to your life. Always expect better things ahead. Never be discouraged. Be part of the cure of the world's ills, rather than part of the disease.

PRAYER FOR THE DAY

I pray that I may keep progressing in the better life. I pray that I may be a part of the forces of good in the world.

Another of the mottoes of this program is "Live and Let Live." This means have tolerance for people who think differently from the way we think, whether they are in our program or outside it. We cannot afford the luxury of being intolerant or critical of others. We do not try to impose our wills on those who differ from us. We are not "holier than thou." We do not have all the answers. We are not better than other good people but live the best we can and allow others to do likewise. *Am I willing to live and let live?*

MEDITATION FOR THE DAY

Learning to know your Higher Power as best you can draws the eternal life nearer to you. Freed from some of the limitations of humanity, you can grow in the things that are eternal. You can strive for what is real and of eternal value. The more you try to live in the consciousness of the unseen world, the gentler will be your passing into it when the time comes. This life is but a preparation for the life to come.

PRAYER FOR THE DAY

I pray that I may live each day as though it were my last. I pray that I may live my life as though it were everlasting.

Another of the mottoes of this program is "Easy Does It." This means that we just go along, doing the best we can and not getting overheated about problems that arise either in the program or outside it. We are excess-prone people, and we have gone to excess in almost everything we have done. We have not been moderate in many things. We have not known how to relax, take things in stride. Faith in a Higher Power can help us learn to take it easy. We are not running the world, and we must ever be aware that each of us is but one among many. *Have I learned to take it easy?*

MEDITATION FOR THE DAY

Human beings, in their troubles and difficulties, need nothing so much as a refuge, a haven where they can lay down their burdens and get relief from their cares. Say to yourself, "God is my refuge." Say it until you are certain of it. Nothing can seriously upset you or cause you fear if your Higher Power is truly your refuge.

PRAYER FOR THE DAY

I pray that I may go each day to God as a refuge until fear goes and peace and security come. I pray that I may feel deeply secure in the haven of His spirit.

SEPTEMBER 8   THOUGHT FOR THE DAY

You will not attend many meetings before you see or hear the phrase "But for the grace of God." Once we have fully accepted the program, we become humble about our achievement. We do not take too much credit for our returned sensibility. When we see another suffering person in the throes of that turmoil, we say to ourselves, "But for the grace of God, there go I." We do not forget the kind of people we were. We remember the people we left behind us, and we are endlessly grateful for the grace of God, which has given us another change. *Am I truly grateful for the grace of God?*

MEDITATION FOR THE DAY

A consciousness of the Higher Power's presence in your life makes all the difference. This consciousness promotes the opening of your whole existence to His influence. It brings wonderful relief from the cares and worries or your daily life. There is peace that passes all understanding, a contentment no person can take away. There is a new freedom and serenity when you walk with Him, in His loving care.

PRAYER FOR THE DAY

I pray that I may walk in God's care. I pray that, as I go, I may feel the spring of God's power in my step and the joy of His love in my heart.

SEPTEMBER 9 THOUGHT FOR THE DAY

We all soon realize the truth of the motto "You Are Not Alone." When people with our affliction are offered a life of freedom from turmoil, will they look at the prospect of living without that distress and ask, "Am I to be consigned to the boredom of some I see? Is there a sufficient substitute?" There is this program with its twelve steps, twelve traditions, and new friends. These prove to newcomers that they are not alone. They have found a sufficient substitute. *Have I found a more than sufficient substitute for my affliction?*

MEDITATION FOR THE DAY

To each of us come moments of despair and doubt that things will ever again be comfortable. We doubt that we can persevere much longer. We wonder if our willingness to trust in a Higher Power is strong enough to see us through these terrible times. At those moments we must rely on faith that God is still there. We must not let these troubling thoughts obscure our communion with God and prayers for His help. Help will come if we do not lose faith.

PRAYER FOR THE DAY

I pray that I may try to rely more fully on the grace of God. I pray that I may be free of doubt in moments of despair.

We are asked how people can live without the past turmoil and be happy. Those things you put in place of your afflictions are more than substitutes for them. One is the fellowship of this group. In this social climate, you find release from care, boredom, tension, and worry. Your vision is cleared, your enthusiasm rekindled. Life will mean something again, and the most rewarding years of your life lie ahead. You will meet lifelong friends in this group. *Does life mean something to me now?*

MEDITATION FOR THE DAY

Do you want the full and complete satisfaction that you find in serving a Higher Power plus all the satisfaction of the world as well? It is not easy to serve two masters and difficult to claim the rewards of both. If you work for God, you will still have great worldly rewards. But you must be prepared to stand apart from that world sometimes. You cannot always turn to the world and expect all the worthy rewards that life has to offer. If you are trying sincerely to serve God, you will have other and greater rewards than the world has to offer.

PRAYER FOR THE DAY

I pray that I may not expect too much from this world. I pray that I may be content with the rewards from serving God.

SEPTEMBER 11   THOUGHT FOR THE DAY

Another part of the answer to how people can live without turmoil and be happy lies in being bound to other members of the group with new ties. They will escape disaster together. New group feeling helps provide them all with a way to identify with each other's common affliction. Each will know what it means to give personally that others may survive and rediscover life. Each will become happy, respected, and useful once more. Since all of this has happened to us, it can happen to them. *Have these things happened to me?*

MEDITATION FOR THE DAY

Some of the words we read in these pages have meanings that go back into remote time. Some of the temptations, the trials we face, have changed very little throughout the history of humankind. God manifests Himself in human lives as strength to resist temptation. The grace of God is that power which enables us to become useful, normal persons. The grace of God is also manifest in love—our love for others, compassion for their problems, and real willingness to help them. The grace of God also manifests itself as peace of mind and serenity. We can have abundant power, love, and serenity in our lives if we ask God for them each day.

PRAYER FOR THE DAY

I pray that I may see God's grace in the strength, love, and serenity in my life. I pray that I may be grateful for the things I have received through the grace of God.

What draws newcomers to this program and offers them hope? They hear the stories of others whose experiences tally with their own. The expressions on the faces of the members, that undefinable something in their eyes are clear testimony. The stimulating atmosphere of the meetings, the undeniable ring of truth in the members' mannerisms all conspire to let the newcomers know that here is a haven at last. They note the practical approach the members take to their problems, the informal atmosphere, the absence of intolerance, and, most conspicuous of all, the uncanny understanding these group members have. *Have I found a real haven in this program?*

MEDITATION FOR THE DAY

Be sensitive to the needs of those you counsel. Be attuned to God's will so that you may fulfill His purposes through your efforts. Be attentive that you further the cause of honesty and unselfishness, of love and earnest desire for spiritual growth. Your life and that of the people you help will be enriched. What had seemed hopeless to one so dejected and remorseful is turned by you as God's servant into new reasons to persevere, to trust, and to embrace the same spirit.

PRAYER FOR THE DAY

I pray that my aspirations for those I help may be attuned to God's will. I pray that I may be His servant in my work with others.

None of us is too discredited or has sunk too low to be welcomed warmly into this program, if we are genuinely seeking. Social distinctions, petty rivalries, personal differences, jealousies are dismissed. Having been all but destroyed by the same forces, whether chemical or others, we are united under a Higher Power. Our hearts and minds are attuned to the well-being of others. There is now little meaning to much of what once mattered most. *Has this program taught me to be truly responsive?*

MEDITATION FOR THE DAY

In time of dire need your Higher Power never fails you. When you call for strength for yourself or for another, it is granted naturally and forcefully. The atmosphere of prayer will move you from despair to reconciliation. It will raise the quality of thought and word and will bring order out of chaos.

PRAYER FOR THE DAY

I pray that I may see violence and conflict changed to peace and simple trust. I pray that I may help bring reconciliation where there is discord.

SEPTEMBER 14 THOUGHT FOR THE DAY

Where there is demand, there is soon supply. Where there is disaster, there is soon relief. Where there is human need for a program, there will soon be a group. That is how this program grows, from little clusters of two, four, more. A visit to a new area by a few older members helps get a new group under way. *Am I doing all I can to spread this program wherever I go?*

MEDITATION FOR THE DAY

How is it possible that a person in dire need of relief seeks more of the same misery? It has happened to us all, and is a characteristic of the compulsive nature of our affliction. If we think of reasons, few will come to light, for the reasons for much of what we do are hidden from consciousness. Only one source of help has ever penetrated that unknown. We call this our Higher Power. We sufferers are given comfort merely by asking.

PRAYER FOR THE DAY

I pray that with more power in my life will also come more faith. I pray that I may come to rely on God more each day.

SEPTEMBER 15   THOUGHT FOR THE DAY

We know only a little about our afflictions and those of others. Do we really fathom the addict's incessant craving, the near-psychotic frustration, or the self-damning guilt? How can you say you feel the alcoholic's withdrawal or know a suicide's feelings? Our Higher Power discloses to us enough that we can make contact with sufferers. We give freely what we know, and we make a life study of this program so that we can pass it on. *Am I always learning about this program so that I may pass it on?*

MEDITATION FOR THE DAY

"In quietness and confidence shall be your strength." Confidence means to have faith in something. We could not live without confidence in others. When you have confidence in God's grace, you can face whatever comes. When you have confidence in God's love, you can be serene and at peace. You can rest in the faith that God will take care of you. Try to rest in God's presence until His life-power flows through you. Be still and in that stillness the still, small Voice will come. It speaks in quietness to the human mind that is attuned to its influence.

PRAYER FOR THE DAY

I pray that I may find strength today in quiet confidence. I pray that I may be content today that God will take care of me.

Let us undertake a short evaluation of the twelve suggested steps of this program. These twelve steps seem to embody five principles. The first step is the membership-requirement step. The second, third, and eleventh steps are the spiritual steps. The fourth, fifth, sixth, seventh, and tenth steps are the personal-inventory steps. The eighth and ninth steps are the restitution steps. The twelfth step is the passing on of the program, or helping others, step. So the five principles are membership requirement, spiritual basis, personal inventory, restitution, and helping others. *Have I made all these steps a part of me?*

MEDITATION FOR THE DAY

We live here and now, as well as in eternity, and our understanding of life determines in some measure how we deal with it. The suffering of another impels us to respond. In this way do we help fruit to grow where there was none. Each time we see a person helped to recovery through our efforts, we are reaffirmed as well.

PRAYER FOR THE DAY

I pray that I may try to make my life a source of energy to a person in need. I pray that I may have something of value to give.

Step One: "We admitted we were powerless over our affliction, that our lives had become unmanageable." This step states the membership requirement of this program. We must admit that our lives are disturbed. We must accept the fact that we are helpless before the power of our affliction. We must admit that we are defeated and that we need help. We must be willing to accept the bitter fact that we are not like normal people in this regard. And we must make, as gracefully as possible, a surrender to the inevitable fact that we must become rational. *Is it difficult for me to admit that I am different from normal individuals?*

MEDITATION FOR THE DAY

"Show Thy ways, O Lord, teach me Thy paths." There seems to be a right way to live and a wrong way. Things work out if we choose the right way. Things work out badly if we choose the wrong way. We seem to take out of life what we put into it. Disobeying the laws of nature makes us unhealthy. Violating moral and spiritual laws makes us unhappy. His path is the one to natural and spiritual health and happiness.

PRAYER FOR THE DAY

I pray that I may try to live the right way. I pray that I may follow the path that leads to a better life.

Step Two: "Came to believe that a Power greater than ourselves could restore us to sanity." Step Three: "Made a decision to turn our will and our lives over to the care of God *as we understood Him.*" Step Eleven: "Sought through prayer and meditation to improve our conscious contact with God as we understood Him, praying only for knowledge of His will for us and the power to carry that out." The fundamental basis of this program is a belief in some Power greater than ourselves. Let us not take this lightly. We cannot fully get the program without this venture of belief. *Have I made the venture of belief in a Power greater than my own?*

MEDITATION FOR THE DAY

There are times when your attention wanders and it is virtually impossible to bring it to bear on some problem. Meditation can help to correct this situation, if you pick a subject in advance. Then when you come to meditate, your thoughts are likely already under way. This program provides an endless number of subjects for meditation, including the steps and traditions. God is close to you in this time of communion. Each day dwell for a while in a place of meditation.

PRAYER FOR THE DAY

I pray that I may train my mind to meditate on the many things I need to consider. I pray that I may be led to fulfill God's plan for my recovery through communion with Him.

SEPTEMBER 19   THOUGHT FOR THE DAY

Let us continue with Steps Two, Three, and Eleven. We must turn to a Higher Power for help, because we are helpless ourselves. When we put our problem in God's hands and leave it there, we have made the most important decision of our lives. From then on we trust our Higher Power for the strength to stay rational. This takes us off the center of the universe and allows us to transfer our problems to a Power outside ourselves. By prayer and meditation we seek to improve our conscious contact with God. We try to live each day the way we believe He wants us to live. *Am I trusting God for the strength to remain rational?*

MEDITATION FOR THE DAY

A spiritual experience is a joyful one. It leads to an understanding of the real meaning of life. It shows you the path to peace. You feel at home in the world when you are in touch with the Divine Spirit. Even a partial realization of the spiritual contact will bring much satisfaction. There is probably no greater comfort than to know that you need never again be tormented, now that God guides your life.

PRAYER FOR THE DAY

I pray that I may find happiness in doing the right thing. I pray that I may find satisfaction in obeying spiritual laws.

Step Four: "Made a searching and fearless moral inventory of ourselves." Step Five: "Admitted to God, to ourselves, and to another human being the exact nature of our wrongs." Step Six: "Were entirely ready to have God remove all these defects of character." Step Seven: "Humbly asked Him to remove our shortcomings." Step Ten: "Continued to take personal inventory and when we were wrong promptly admitted it." In taking a personal inventory, we have to be absolutely honest with ourselves and with other people. *Have I taken an honest inventory of myself?*

MEDITATION FOR THE DAY

We can believe that God can bring order from chaos, good from evil, peace from turmoil. We give Him our cares willingly in exchange for His goodness to us. If it is of God, it must be good. Honesty, purity, unselfishness, and love are of God. In living as He would have us live, we remain safe and at peace in His loving care.

PRAYER FOR THE DAY

I pray that I may reach out for the good in life. I pray that I may choose those things which help me to remain safe and at peace.

SEPTEMBER 21   THOUGHT FOR THE DAY

Let us continue with Steps Four, Five, Six, Seven, and Ten. In taking a personal inventory of ourselves, we have to face facts as they are. We have to stop running away. We must face reality. We must see ourselves as we truly are. We must admit our faults openly and try to correct them. We must try to see where we have been dishonest, impure, selfish, and unloving. This is a constant process day by day since the threat of turmoil is always present. *Am I taking a daily inventory of myself?*

MEDITATION FOR THE DAY

Our Higher Power cannot be perceived with our usual senses. It takes an act of faith, a venture of belief, to realize Him. The evidence of His existence abounds in people who have received from faith a recovery from their malady or reconciliation to abstinence. He suspends all manner of threats, turmoil, madness, or death if we but have faith. We believe, and we are safe from harm.

PRAYER FOR THE DAY

I pray that I may make the great venture of belief. I pray that my perception may not be blocked by intellectual pride or paranoid distrust.

Step Eight: "Made a list of all persons we had harmed, and became willing to make amends to them all." Step Nine: "Made direct amends to such people wherever possible, except when to do so would injure them or others." Making restitution for the wrongs we have done is often very difficult. It hurts our pride, that seemingly insurmountable barrier. But the rewards are great. It takes courage to apologize, but the results more than justify it. An enemy may become a friend, and a weight lifted. *Have I done my best to make all the restitution possible?*

MEDITATION FOR THE DAY

There should be joy in living the spiritual life. A faith without joy is not genuine. If you are not happier as a result of your faith, there is probably something wrong with it. What happens on the surface of your life is not important. Faith gives you a deeper reward. Each day offers joy, with life abundant and outreaching.

PRAYER FOR THE DAY

I pray that my horizons may grow wider. I pray that I may keep reaching out for more service and companionship.

Step Twelve: "Having had a spiritual awakening as the result of these steps, we tried to carry this message to others, and to practice these principles in all our affairs." Note that the basis of our effectiveness in carrying the message to others is the reality of our own spiritual awakening. If we have not changed, we cannot be used to change others. To keep this program, we must pass it on, give it away. We cannot hoard it for ourselves. If it flows into us and then stops, it will die. It must continue to flow out of us as it flows into us. *Am I always ready to give away what I have learned in this program?*

MEDITATION FOR THE DAY

When you are faced with a problem beyond your strength, you must turn to the Higher Power by an act of faith. It is that turning to Him in each trying situation that you must cultivate. You must have faith that you will benefit by your trust, overcoming reluctance, pride, fear. Your appeal will be received generously. God's grace will enter your life. Yours will be the power to face trials, the ability to comfort others, and the secure feeling that He is with you.

PRAYER FOR THE DAY

I pray that I may try to draw near to God each day in prayer. I pray that I may feel His nearness and His strength in my life.

Let us continue with Step Twelve: We must "practice these principles in all our affairs." This really means carrying on the entire program. We practice these principles not just with respect to our affliction but in *all* our affairs. We do not give one part of our lives to the Higher Power and keep the other parts to ourselves. We must unselfishly give our whole lives to Him, trying to do His will in every respect. This is the embodiment of the program, the fulfillment, with all the promise of the future in it—an ever-widening horizon. *Do I carry the principles of the program with me wherever I go?*

MEDITATION FOR THE DAY

We emancipate our inner selves through the awakening of our spirit and by following the principles of this program. We are renewed, for we know the real joy of being alive once again. Each time we talk to others about our recovery or see others who have recovered, we have proof beyond doubt of what God's spirit can accomplish in our lives. Accident it cannot be, for those who again fall victim to their affliction can recover once more if they return. God's spirit says to heart and mind and soul, "Do this and live."

PRAYER FOR THE DAY

I pray that I may follow the dictates of my conscience. I pray that I may follow the inner urge to do, to grow, to persist.

Let us consider the term "spiritual experience." It is something that brings about a personality change. We surrender our lives to a Higher Power. In so doing, we are changed. The nature of this change is evident in the members of our group. The change is not necessarily sudden and spectacular, though it could be and has been. We do not gain an overwhelming God-consciousness in a flash, followed by abrupt changes of feelings and outlook. It is most often subtle, gradual, continuing. *Do I see a gradual and continuing change in myself?*

MEDITATION FOR THE DAY

For rest from the cares of life you can turn to God each day in prayer and meditation. Real relaxation and serenity come from a deep sense of the fundamental goodness of the universe. Commune with Him for rest. Rely on His will. Accept His purpose in and for your life. Nourish within you the eager enthusiasm and gratitude that this spiritual experience affords you.

PRAYER FOR THE DAY

I pray that others may share in this spiritual experience. I pray that I may continue to change and grow.

Most of our spiritual experiences are of the educational variety, and they develop slowly over a period of time. Though immediate God-consciousness is frequent enough, it is more likely that friends of newcomers will be aware of the difference long before they are themselves. There finally comes a profound realization of personal change, an alteration in attitude toward life that certainly could not have been brought about by themselves alone. We know that it is the work of our Higher Power. *Is my outlook on life changing for the better?*

MEDITATION FOR THE DAY

Look at the world as your Father's house. You are a servant to all who reside there. No work is beneath you, no responsibility too great. Remember the help you sought from others that you now can easily give to them. Show them the spiritual experience as it has altered you. It is your Father's expression of love through you to them.

PRAYER FOR THE DAY

I pray that I may serve others out of gratitude to God. I pray that my work may be a small repayment for His grace so freely given to me.

Concerning spiritual experience, what often takes place in a few months could seldom if ever have been accomplished by years of self-discipline. As stated in the A.A. program: "With few exceptions our members find that they have tapped an unsuspected inner resource which they presently identify with their own conception of a Power greater than themselves. Most of us think this awareness of a Power greater than ourselves is the essence of spiritual experience." We are not the only suffering beings in whom God-consciousness occurs. *Have I tapped the inner resource that can change my life?*

MEDITATION FOR THE DAY

The power of God's grace is limited only by your understanding and will. His miracle evolves with the spiritual vision of the soul. God respects free will. Our inner distortions and uncontrolled outbreaks when we were distressed showed a negative will. Our Higher Power restored us when our desire gave Him the opportunity to do so.

PRAYER FOR THE DAY

I pray that I may not limit God's power by refusing to open my mind to His influence. I pray that I may keep my mind open today to His influence.

SEPTEMBER 28   THOUGHT FOR THE DAY

While we have all experienced turmoil, we cannot give you what we felt. We can only share what we have learned with you, knowing that this is the key you have sought. Here is the indescribable value of this program, this giving to those who are as we were the awesome yet simple solution. Accept faith in a Higher Power, and be certain that you will never again be alone. One day soon you will give it all to someone else, when that call comes to you. *Am I able to see that I am a part of a continuum of human salvation?*

MEDITATION FOR THE DAY

We are to meditate, and that means to think deeply, to ponder for some purpose or goal. Some new members find the idea of meditation painful, even a near-impossibility. Be thankful that you can read these words. Some can envy you that ability. In thinking of yourself, of what you have come to be, is it not wiser to be charitable than ruthless? Guilt will destroy. Hate is dangerous. Neither begets peace. Meditate in love and honesty, and faith.

PRAYER FOR THE DAY

I pray that I may accept everything I had become. I pray that I may become everything I accept.

SEPTEMBER 29   THOUGHT FOR THE DAY

Having come through nine months of the year, we pause and ask ourselves some questions, as the inventory steps suggest. Just how good a member am I? Am I attending meetings? Am I doing my share to carry the load? If there is work to be done, do I volunteer? Will I speak before a group, or chair a meeting when asked? If a Twelfth Step call comes to me, do I respond and follow through? My daily life should be a living demonstration of the principles of this program. *Am I an effective member who lives this program?*

MEDITATION FOR THE DAY

I questioned how I gain the strength to be effective and to accept responsibility. I ask the Higher Power for that strength each day. Like countless others, every day I live I revel in the knowledge that the necessary power shall be given to me. For every task, every critical challenge, the necessary strength to achieve success is there. To gain more, I have but to give more.

PRAYER FOR THE DAY

I pray that I may accept every task as a challenge. I pray that I may remember that I cannot fail with God's strength within me.

There are no true leaders in this program. There are those who volunteer to accept responsibility. The work of carrying on the program, leading group meetings, doing the work, speaking to groups, doing Twelfth Step calls are things I do on a voluntary basis. If I don't volunteer to do something concrete for the program, the movement is that much less effective. *Am I doing my share for this program?*

MEDITATION FOR THE DAY

Arise from a temporary reversal and go forward with assurance that, once you have rejoined us, your confidence will return. You have made the right decision by returning. You know that you are not alone. Think long and hard about how easily it happened. Do you wonder any longer why we are told that we are never cured? Even now you may have learned a vital lesson in recovery, despite anguish, guilt, and misery. That you have a chance for recovery, with His guidance and strength, should be proof that God does indeed watch over you.

PRAYER FOR THE DAY

I pray that I may be touched again by the healing hand of God. I pray that I may not falter or grope in darkness ever again.

OCTOBER 1   THOUGHT FOR THE DAY

This program will lose some of its effectiveness if I do not do my share. Are there some things I do not feel like doing? Am I held back by self-consciousness or fear? Self-consciousness is a form of pride. It is a form of fear that something may happen to me. What happens to me is not all that important. The others see my sincerity and honesty of purpose rather than how well I do the work. *Am I holding back because I am afraid of not making a good impression?*

MEDITATION FOR THE DAY

Look to God for the true power that will make you effective. That is the secret of a truly effective life. You will be used to help others find effectiveness. Failures come from depending too much on your own strength. Self-analysis can be turned into self-depreciation, which is a betrayal of mental honesty in a very real and damaging sense. To be effective, rely on God's strength.

PRAYER FOR THE DAY

I pray that I may feel that nothing is too much for me through God's strength. I pray that I may be effective through His guidance.

OCTOBER 2   THOUGHT FOR THE DAY

What makes an effective talk at a group meeting? It is not a fine speech with a careful choice of words and an impressive delivery. Often a few simple words direct from the heart are more effective than the most polished speech. There is always a temptation to speak beyond your own experience in order to make a good impression. This is never effective. What does not come from the heart does not reach the heart. What comes from personal experience and a sincere desire to help others reaches the heart. *Do I speak with a deep desire to help?*

MEDITATION FOR THE DAY

"Thy will be done." That must be your oft-repeated prayer. And in the words you say to others, they sense His will reflected in your sincerity, your message. If you are honestly trying to live your life as God wills you to live, others will know it. Those who follow the will of God may not inherit the earth, but they will inherit real peace of mind.

PRAYER FOR THE DAY

I pray that I may follow the will of God for my life. I pray that my life will help lead others to peace of mind.

OCTOBER 3 THOUGHT FOR THE DAY

How do I approach new prospects? Am I always try-ing to dominate the conversation? Do I tend to lay down the law about what they must do? Do I judge them privately and feel they have small chance of making the program? Do I belittle them to myself? Or am I willing to bare my soul to encourage them to talk about themselves? And then am I willing to be a genuine listener, not interrupting but hearing them to the end? Do I feel a genuine oneness with them in their desire to recover? *Will I do all I can to help them along the path to recovery?*

MEDITATION FOR THE DAY

"The work of righteousness shall be peace, and the effect of righteousness shall be quietness and assur-ance forever." Only when the soul attains this calm can there be true spiritual work done and mind and soul and body be strong to conquer and bear all things. Peace is the result of righteousness. There is no peace in wrongdoing, but if we live the way God wants us to live, quietness and assurance follow. As-surance is that calmness born of a deep certainty of God's strength available to us and in His power to love and guard us from all harm and wrongdoing.

PRAYER FOR THE DAY

I pray that I may attain a state of true calmness. I pray that I may live in quietness and peace.

OCTOBER 4   THOUGHT FOR THE DAY

Am I critical of other members of my group or of new prospects? Do I ever say about other members: "I don't think they're really sincere. I think they're bluffing and aren't really following the program." Do I realize that my doubts show and are hurting those members? With that attitude I betray my own insecurity and hurt others' chances for recovery. *Is my attitude always constructive, never destructive?*

MEDITATION FOR THE DAY

A wonderful illumination of thought is given to those who are guided by God's spirit. To those who are materialistic, there is nothing in God or a finer life to appeal to them. But to those who are guided by the spirit, there is strength, peace, and calm in communion with God. There is companionship with others. There is real meaning and purpose in life.

PRAYER FOR THE DAY

I pray that I may be guided by the spirit of God. I pray that I may feel His presence in my life.

OCTOBER 5   THOUGHT FOR THE DAY

Do I realize how subtly intolerance and disguised resentment can creep into my attitude toward fellow members or other groups? Am I critical of the way others think or act? Do I broadcast criticisms of other groups? Do I realize that all members, no matter what their limitations, have something to offer the group? Even if I do not agree with their procedure, do I believe that they have a rightful place in this program if they follow its traditions? *Am I tolerant of persons and groups?*

MEDITATION FOR THE DAY

Every visit to help others, every unselfish effort to assist can be blessed by the Higher Power. In our group the contribution we make, whether it be profoundly moving testimony or a gentle smile, can be a blessing to those who are suffering. Led by the spirit of God, we can be tolerant, sympathetic, and understanding of others and so accomplish much.

PRAYER FOR THE DAY

I pray that I may be led by the spirit of God. I pray that I may be tolerant and accepting of others.

OCTOBER 6   THOUGHT FOR THE DAY

Is it my desire to be a big shot in my group? Do I always want to be in the limelight, directing the meeting, taking it upon myself to run things? Do I feel that no one else can do as good a job as I can? Leadership qualities are fine, provided they are employed for the right reasons. Part of the purpose of this program is to develop new members to carry it on. We are followers of a program, not leaders of a movement. *Do I know that the group will carry on without me, if it needs to?*

MEDITATION FOR THE DAY

Belief in a God of our understanding can help to make us truly grateful and humble. Since we cannot see God, we must believe in Him without seeing. What we can see clearly is the change in human beings who have sincerely asked God for the strength to change. The change continues with time, provided they maintain the relationship with God that causes change.

PRAYER FOR THE DAY

I pray that I may believe that God will change me. I pray that I will always be willing for Him to change me for the better.

OCTOBER 7   THOUGHT FOR THE DAY

During our first weeks at meetings all of us learn the
Serenity Prayer. At first it seems like a riddle. "God
grant me the serenity to accept the things I cannot
change." That seems impossible. Accept my affliction
and my powerlessness over it? "Courage to change
the things I can." That also seems impossible. Courage to face the task of making over my life? "Wisdom
to know the difference." Would that I were so wise!
The answer lies in the first three words, "God grant
me." What I cannot do, God can do. *Have I faith that
God can grant me so much?*

MEDITATION FOR THE DAY

You must always remember that you are weak but
God is strong. God knows all about your weakness.
He hears every cry for mercy, every sigh of weariness, every plea for help, every lament over failure.
But we truly fail only when we trust too much in our
own strength, not when we acknowledge our weakness. Then God's strength is given to us.

PRAYER FOR THE DAY

I pray that I may learn to trust in God for strength. I
pray that He may grant me serenity, courage, and
wisdom.

OCTOBER 8   THOUGHT FOR THE DAY

Do I put too much reliance on any one member of my group? Do I set that person on a pedestal to be worshiped? If so, my house is built upon sand. I can do the same thing if I try to champion my group above all others or criticize those who start a new group. The role of a good member is to champion not one leader or group but the program itself. Groups change and grow, form new groups, change direction. *Can I accept changes in my group, knowing that the program itself is changeless and enduring?*

MEDITATION FOR THE DAY

When we think of God, our doubts and fears, hurts and resentments leave us. They are replaced by love and outflowing faith that will sustain us no matter where we are. There is no dependence on personalities or surroundings. Our faith sustains us in any surrounding.

PRAYER FOR THE DAY

I pray that I may not forget that I came to God at a time of great turmoil. I pray that my faith will sustain me wherever I may be.

OCTOBER 9　　THOUGHT FOR THE DAY

Groups have problems as they grow over the years, just as people do. Am I willing to be bored sometimes by what I feel are repetitious and flavorless meetings? Do I listen willingly to a long-winded story in lurid detail? Do I realize that lives of new members may be changed by the words that bore me? Do I realize that the speaker may be helped by the opportunity to share his story? My boredom will pass, but what that person is saying may well be the beginning of a new life. *Am I willing to be patient for the good of another?*

MEDITATION FOR THE DAY

God would draw us all closer to Him in the bonds of the spirit. Each experience of our life, of joy, of sorrow, of danger, of safety, of difficulty, of success, of hardship, of ease—each should be accepted as part of our common lot, in the bonds of the spirit.

PRAYER FOR THE DAY

I pray that I may be drawn closer to God in the bonds of the spirit. I pray that I may look for the good in the bonds of true fellowship.

"You are not alone." When new members come into my group, do I make a special effort to make them feel at home? Do I put myself out to listen to them, even if their ideas of this program are very vague? Do I make it a habit to talk to new members, or do I leave that to others? I may not be able to help them, but then again it might be something that I say that would help start them on the road to recovery. Seeing new members sitting alone, do I try to talk with them or join my own special circle and leave them out? *Are all new members my responsibility?*

MEDITATION FOR THE DAY

Nobody likes the servant who avoids extra work, who complains about being called from one task to do a less enjoyable one. View your day's work by thinking about how God wants you to do it, never shirking any responsibility and often going out of your way to be of service.

PRAYER FOR THE DAY

I pray that I may be a good servant. I pray that I may be willing to go out of my way to be a friend.

OCTOBER 11 THOUGHT FOR THE DAY

How good a sponsor am I? When I have brought new members to a meeting, do I feel that my responsibility has ended? Or do I make it my job to stay with them through thick and thin, until they have become steady members or have found other sponsors? If they don't come to meetings, do I say to myself, "Well, they've been told all about the program. If they don't want it, there's nothing I can do." Or do I try to find out whether there is another reason for their absence? Do I go out of my way to find out if there is anything more I can do to help? *Am I doing a good job of being a sponsor?*

MEDITATION FOR THE DAY

If I hold resentment against others that I find difficult to overcome, I should try to put something else constructive into my mind. I should pray for those against whom I hold the resentment. I should put them in God's hands and let Him show the way. If it proves that they are doing the same for me, we are all in God's grace.

PRAYER FOR THE DAY

I pray that I may see something good in every person, even those I dislike. I pray that He open my eyes to make me aware of others in His domain.

OCTOBER 12   THOUGHT FOR THE DAY

Am I still a new member who is relatively uninvolved? Am I taking a "free ride" in group activities and remaining in the background? If so, I must realize that I am not really in the program, nor am I likely to get much out of it. I hear the advice, "Easy does it—but do it." Those who helped me when I needed it were doers who did not remain in the background. *Am I a doer in this program?*

MEDITATION FOR THE DAY

Try to be thankful for whatever vision you have. Try to perform, in the little things, faithful service to God and others. Do your small part every day in a spirit of service to God. Be a doer of God's word, not a hearer only. In your daily life try to keep faith with God. Every day brings a new opportunity to be of some use. Even when you are tempted to rest or let things go or to evade the issue, make it a habit to meet the issue squarely as a challenge and not to hold back.

PRAYER FOR THE DAY

I pray that I may perform each task faithfully. I pray that I may meet each issue of life squarely and not hold back.

OCTOBER 13   THOUGHT FOR THE DAY

When we are relatively new in the program, we have a feeling of well-being, of having reached a haven. We tend to become complacent as time goes on if we do not begin to participate more actively, to help the group and to grow ourselves. There is that time for every member when the nervousness and confusion are no longer adequate excuses. Was it not terrifying to be called upon to lead a meeting the first time? "Train-along" is a means of introducing beginners to Twelfth Step work. We accompany an experienced member on calls to prospects. It is a useful way to participate and mature. *Has the time come for me to volunteer?*

MEDITATION FOR THE DAY

The growth of God's kingdom is slow but steady. We keep striving for something better. We acknowledge the three A's—*acceptance, awareness, action*. Acceptance began when we took Step One. Awareness of God, of ourselves, of others deepens with every day of recovery. Action comes where we act upon our will. We rely on God to inspire the will and motivate the action.

PRAYER FOR THE DAY

I pray that God may inspire me always to be willing to grow. I pray that I may keep climbing the rungs of the ladder of recovery.

OCTOBER 14   THOUGHT FOR THE DAY

How big a part of my life is this program? Is it just one of my activities? Do I go to meetings only occasionally? Do I hesitate to mention the program to others, wary of what they will think of me? If I feel that the program is the foundation of my recovery, and if I honestly realize that I would be in trouble without it, there is no room for hesitation. A group cannot survive without active members. Tradition One says, "Our common welfare should come first; personal recovery depends upon our unity." We cannot afford to be reluctant about our involvement. Others depend upon us for support, for active participation. *Am I proud of my involvement with this program?*

MEDITATION FOR THE DAY

Lay upon God your failures and mistakes and shortcomings. Do not dwell upon them, or upon your past behavior. You need not fear being criticized for faith and hope for a better life. When you strive to help others, you are doing God's work.

PRAYER FOR THE DAY

I pray that I will not withdraw from life's challenges out of fear of failure. I pray that I may trust in God to help me achieve a better life.

OCTOBER 15 THOUGHT FOR THE DAY

Am I deeply grateful to this program for what it has done for me? Through it I have regained rationality and have opened up an entirely new life for myself. It has made it possible for me to follow other interests, in work and in associations with others. It has made a full life possible for me, because I take it with me wherever I go. *Do I realize how much I owe this program?*

MEDITATION FOR THE DAY

There is only one way to get full satisfaction from life, and that is to live the way you believe your Higher Power wants you to live. If you persist in a life with God, you will have the sense of being on the right road. Whatever the obstacles, the power of God will provide ways to overcome them.

PRAYER FOR THE DAY

I pray that I may have a sense of the eternal value of the work I do. I pray that I may work not only for today but also for eternity.

OCTOBER 16   THOUGHT FOR THE DAY

How seriously do I take my obligations to this program? Have I taken all the good but let my obligations slide? Tradition Five says, "Each group has but one primary purpose—to carry its message to the person who still suffers." Am I grateful enough for what I have been given to give it to those who need it, those who are suffering as I once suffered? Giving it away is a vital part of this program. *Do I feel that I owe the program my loyalty and devotion?*

MEDITATION FOR THE DAY

If your heart is right, your world will be right. The beginning of all reform must be in yourself. It is not what happens to you but how you take it that matters. There is a slogan, "Have an attitude of gratitude." It helps when you turn to your inner self and be grateful that something is there that you were not aware of when you were suffering. It is the spirit of God.

PRAYER FOR THE DAY

I pray that my inner person will continue to be healed. I pray that the spirit of God will help me to be free.

OCTOBER 17 THOUGHT FOR THE DAY

One of the defects most of us share is procrastination. It may be a part of our affliction, or it may be a universal trait. We seem to be unable to attack a problem actively. We can think and talk about it endlessly but do not open the door to action. There is a motto for us: "Utilize, don't analyze." Don't "review" the Twelve Steps; work them. Too much self-evaluation can drive away the incentive for action. *Am I thinking too much and doing too little?*

MEDITATION FOR THE DAY

Today I will look up to God, not down at myself. I will look away from the unpleasant past, the ugliness, the imperfections in the world. In my unrest I will see God's calmness. With His help my spirit will grow and my aspirations will soar skyward. I will be enabled to do what seemed too hard for me before.

PRAYER FOR THE DAY

I pray that I may keep my eyes trained on God, above the horizon of myself. I pray that this new vision of life will heal my troubled memory and strengthen my will to act.

OCTOBER 18   THOUGHT FOR THE DAY

Have I recovered from my oversensitivity, my too easily hurt feelings, and my laziness? Am I willing to go all out for this program, no matter what the cost to my creature comforts? Is my convenience no longer my first concern? Do I begin to hear the silent cries from others? Can I ignore my embarrassment or discomfort if things need to be done for the good of others who need this program? I am educating myself about what I need to do for others. *Am I willing to give what is needed when it is needed?*

MEDITATION FOR THE DAY

Humility arises from a deep sense of gratitude to God for giving you the strength to rise above past failures. Humility is not inconsistent with self-respect. You can have self-respect and respect for others and yet be humble. The humble person is tolerant of others and accepts their foibles and shortcomings. He sees God's spirit moving in their lives, as in his own.

PRAYER FOR THE DAY

I pray that I may be truly humble and yet have self-respect. I pray that I may see the good in myself and in others.

OCTOBER 19   THOUGHT FOR THE DAY

Most of us in this program have experienced the disdain of onlookers who say that we are wasting our time—"the blind leading the blind." In commercial and professional circles this criticism is also heard, however subtly offered. Yet are we all not living proof of the success of the blind leading the blind, knowing that our Higher Power gives us sight? What group has more compassion, more intimate knowledge, more insight about the problems than ours? Who has more at stake than our members? If "sight" alone succeeded, why have so many "sighted" ones failed where our members succeeded? *Do I dismiss the criticism of those who would harm this program?*

MEDITATION FOR THE DAY

We know that the cry of the human soul is never unheard by God. He hears the cry, even if we fail to notice His response. The cry must always evoke a response in God. It may be that our failure to discern properly keeps us unaware of the response. But the grace of God is always available for every human being who sincerely calls for help. We see God's response in the changed lives about us.

PRAYER FOR THE DAY

I pray that I may trust God to answer my prayers as He sees fit. I pray that I may discern His response and be content with whatever form His response may take.

The moment we become aware that this program has something to offer those who have not found help elsewhere, we are compelled to face Tradition Three: "The only requirement for membership is a desire to recover from this affliction." That tradition, along with Step One, is absolutely essential to success in this program. Half the battle is admitting the problem exists. We cannot recover if we do not realize that we are ill. *Do I know that I must start with first things first?*

MEDITATION FOR THE DAY

In whatever challenges we face in recovery, not my will but Thy will be done. Many times things turn out differently from what we would like, but usually for the best in the long run, if it is the result of the guidance we asked the Higher Power to give us. How many times did things turn out disastrously for us before, when we refused to ask for guidance? In the long term we will know that God's will for us is right for us.

PRAYER FOR THE DAY

I pray that I may see the working of God's will in my life. I pray that I may be content with what He has in store for me.

As an outgrowth of my experience with this program, I now understand myself better than I did before. I have learned what was the matter with me, and I know a lot about what makes me tick. I know I will never be alone again. I am one of many who have this affliction, and I know that I can do something about it. I have accepted that I am not different, and I have found my rightful place in the world. *Am I beginning to understand how I got this way and who I am?*

MEDITATION FOR THE DAY

"Behold, I stand at the door, and knock: if any man hear My voice, and open the door, I will come in to him and will sup with him, and he with Me." This profound entrance of God's spirit into our lives is ours for the asking. We spent years of time suffering for every kind of reason before we learned to listen for the gentle knock. Then we opened the door of our heart and let God's spirit come in. Would we have it any other way?

PRAYER FOR THE DAY

I pray that I may let God's spirit come into my life. I pray that I may know His endless peace.

Another reward of this program is that I can now have ease of mind, knowing that the rest of my life can be free of turmoil. I hope that I have no more reservations, no more doubts, now that I have surrendered as fully as possible to this promise. I know that this promise requires some response from me: no excuses, no pretenses, no backsliding. For me the bomb is defused, the explosion won't occur, and I will always be safe—unless I reactivate that bomb again. *Am I fully resigned to this fact about my life?*

MEDITATION FOR THE DAY

Day by day we build an unshakable faith in a Higher Power and in His ability to give us all the help we need. We did not reach the depths of despair overnight, nor will we acquire the serenity and capacity to shrug off the threat of disaster in a few days. Our lives are not over until they are lived. With God's help, we shall live them out as He wills us to live, safely, sanely, at peace.

PRAYER FOR THE DAY

I pray that I may build an unshakable faith in God. I pray that I may live my life in accordance with His will for me.

OCTOBER 23 THOUGHT FOR THE DAY

We who read these thoughts share many of the same circumstances that brought us here. Younger readers cope with no greater and no smaller challenges than the older ones. This program does not differentiate because of age, nor does it spoon-feed the steps. Honesty is the same at fifteen and at sixty-five. Facing facts and acknowledging our affliction get no easier with age. *Am I convinced that age is irrelevant to the value of this program?*

MEDITATION FOR THE DAY

Though it may seem a paradox, if we are going to live fully, we must believe in spiritual forces that we cannot see more than in material things that we can see. This is not really a contradiction. We accept electricity as a force, though we cannot see it. We see its force in the material things it empowers—the lamp, the stove, the clock. We accept the spirit of God in the same way. Though we cannot see it, we see its power in changed human lives, in the change from despair to hope, insanity to rationality. A changed life is brought about by spiritual forces working within us.

PRAYER FOR THE DAY

I pray that God may help me to live fully now, today. I pray that I may believe in the unseen spirit of God.

We soon realize in this program that our kinship with a Higher Power is of paramount importance to our recovery. This is borne out by Tradition Two: "For our group purpose there is but one ultimate authority —a loving God as He may express Himself in our group conscience. Our leaders are but trusted servants—they do not govern." In this program we are all equal. We accept the responsibility for ourselves and for self-government. *Am I ready to be responsible for myself?*

MEDITATION FOR THE DAY

Although we cannot see spiritual forces, we can call upon those forces to help us work for change. There are many things in life that we can work to modify. Through discussion, meditation, sponsorship, and prayer we can do a great deal to change what may have seemed an unchangeable situation. Wonderful things can be done, if we are willing to ask for God's help and guidance each step of the way.

PRAYER FOR THE DAY

I pray that I may accept God as the ultimate authority. I pray that I may use responsibly the power He grants to me.

OCTOBER 25   THOUGHT FOR THE DAY

I have learned to live one day at a time. I have finally realized the astounding fact that all I have is *now*. This realization sweeps away all vain regret and makes my thoughts of the future free of terror. Now is mine. I can do with it as I will, for better or worse. Here is my life—what I do in this moment. The rest of my life is a succession of other "nows." I have this moment by the grace of God, and what I do with it or fail to do will make or break me. *Am I aware that my life is now?*

MEDITATION FOR THE DAY

We should work at overcoming ourselves, our ego-centeredness and our selfish desires. We can never fully attain unselfishness. But we can come to accept that we are not at the center of the universe, with the world spinning around us. We can at least make the effort to conquer the self-like and seek daily to obtain more and more of this self-conquest. "He that over-comes himself is greater than he who conquers a city."

PRAYER FOR THE DAY

I pray that I may strive to overcome my self-importance. I pray that I may achieve a true perspective of my significance in the world.

OCTOBER 26 THOUGHT FOR THE DAY

Somewhere within a reasonable distance there is usually a meeting I can go to. If not, I can find one or two members to talk to—and that's a meeting. Where else would I find the understanding, the fellowship, the companionship this program offers? I am no longer a homeless nomad. I have a place to go and a message to give. *Do I thank God every day for a meeting to attend and members to be with?*

MEDITATION FOR THE DAY

Remember that at every meeting there is always One present without Whom we would have no hope. Our Higher Power would have us meet with Him whenever possible. Where we meet—in a home, an office, a hospital, a jail—is not important. We are together, and He is there with us.

PRAYER FOR THE DAY

I pray that I may regularly meet with God and my fellows. I pray that God's presence may assure us that we are at home.

OCTOBER 27   THOUGHT FOR THE DAY

I can help others who share my affliction. I am of some use in the world. I have a purpose in life. I am worth something at last. My life has a direction and a meaning it never had before. All that feeling of utter futility is gone. God has given me a new lease on life. Others need the help I can give. He has helped me survive all the hazards of the past. He has brought me to a place of real usefulness in the world. This is my opportunity. *Having had my life saved, will I give of it now to this program?*

MEDITATION FOR THE DAY

All of us have our own battles to win. One battle is between the material and spiritual views of life. Something must guide us. Will it be wealth, pride, selfishness, greed? Or will it be faith, honesty, love, unselfishness, and service? Each of us has a choice. We can choose the material or the spiritual. We cannot put both first in our lives. We must keep striving until we win the battle. When we win the victory, we can believe that God will rejoice with us.

PRAYER FOR THE DAY

I pray that I may make the right choice. I pray that I may keep striving until the battle is won.

Each of the groups does for its members what all the others do. The program operates on the same premises, whatever the group. Our program is adapted from the A.A. program and is similar to other programs based on A.A. We will describe much of this program in the coming days. To start: Our problems do not differ much from group to group. Members have the same common affliction. The circumstances may differ, just as people differ. But for all practical purposes our kinds of problems are alike. *Do I realize that my affliction is very much like that of fellow group members everywhere?*

MEDITATION FOR THE DAY

In the quest for understanding, we often search in ways that yield no insight, no help, no hope. This is the blind-alley approach. Sometimes we spend time with others who try to retrain our thinking so that we will be like them. That is the brain-washing approach. When we come into this program, we become aware of a Higher Power and the amazing ways in which faith performs miracles in us. All the false paths are forgotten. This becomes the first day of the rest of our lives.

PRAYER FOR THE DAY

I pray that I may help those afflicted as I was helped. I pray that I may lead them to Him, just as I was led.

OCTOBER 29   THOUGHT FOR THE DAY

We say that our affliction is a disease. It is a spiritual illness as well. Most patients in mental hospitals lack spiritual awareness. We can learn this lack has little to do with medicine, diet, treatment, or physical disorders. Some groups have in their membership former mental patients. By contrast they display liveliness, buoyancy, spirit. If they were asked, they would tell you that their manner relates to an awakening of God-consciousness and a newfound faith. *Am I aware that my affliction was also a spiritual one?*

MEDITATION FOR THE DAY

Our true measure of success in life is the measure of spiritual progress that we have revealed in our lives. Others should be able to see a demonstration of God's will in how we live. The measure of His will is the measure of our true success. We can do our best to be a demonstration each day of the power of God in human lives, an example of the working out of the grace of God in the hearts of men and women.

PRAYER FOR THE DAY

I pray that I may so live that others will see in me the working out of the will of God. I pray that my whole life may be a demonstration of what the will of God can do.

Our affliction is the same in all members. Only super-
ficial details vary. That is evident to most observers,
but it is often difficult for victims to accept. It forces us
to acknowledge that some have recovered. That
means that we can recover, too, if we are willing to
take certain difficult steps. Those steps are not taken
quickly or effortlessly or without anguish for some.
*Am I able to face the challenges this program puts before
me?*

MEDITATION FOR THE DAY

There is a time for everything. We should learn to
wait patiently until the right time comes. "One day at
a time." We waste our energies trying to get things
done before we are ready. The hard lesson is patience. If it is part of God's plan that we face painful
truths about ourselves, we will need faith, fortitude,
and patience.

PRAYER FOR THE DAY

I pray that I may not expect to have things until I have
earned the right to them. I pray that I may have patience based on the assurance that God will help me
work changes in my life as he helped me recover.

Our affliction is characterized by painful symptoms. We know how agonizing the affliction can become, but not until we begin this program do we fully realize how near hopeless our situation had become. We were like those now in other, similar programs— lost, near death of body and spirit. *Am I aware that I share with many others the agony of affliction—and more, the joy of recovery through programs like this one?*

MEDITATION FOR THE DAY

In all of us is the potentiality for failure or for success. As persons who have tasted the bitterness of failure, we realize that people seldom value a thing until it is lost to them. Our lives are endowed through a Higher Power with the miracle of another chance. Staggered by the odds against success in recovery, we call on God to quell unrest and fear and grant us courage to persist.

PRAYER FOR THE DAY

I pray that I may never turn a deaf ear to the encouragement so vital to my recovery. I pray that I may listen for God's reassurance.

NOVEMBER 1 THOUGHT FOR THE DAY

We all know what happens to a tooth once a cavity starts and nothing is done about it. In time the tooth is rotted beyond hope. In some respects that is what happens to the person whose affliction is not arrested. The deterioration is progressive, often leading to death. But most afflictions like ours can be arrested. All that is needed is the desire for recovery. Then, in this program, we gain first the hope of recovery and finally satisfaction and contentment in the fact of recovery. *Have I found contentment in my recovery in this program?*

MEDITATION FOR THE DAY

Faith is the messenger that bears your prayers to God. Prayer can be like incense, rising ever higher and higher. The prayer of faith is the prayer of trust, which feels the presence of God that it rises to meet. It can be sure of some response from God. We can say a prayer of thanks to God every day for His grace, which has kept us on the right way and allowed us to start living the good life. We should pray to God with faith and trust and gratitude.

PRAYER FOR THE DAY

I pray that my affliction is a thing of the past. I pray that my faith will continue my course upward.

NOVEMBER 2   THOUGHT FOR THE DAY

Not until I had real faith in a Higher Power did He grant me insight about myself. I discovered that my problems began in a deep selfishness that made it impossible for me to be able to feel love. Nor could I love myself. Trust, self-confidence, hope—all were missing because I could not love. It is said that we must love ourselves for we are His children. One who cannot do so can hardly know how to love others. *Do I remember that to love others I must love myself?*

MEDITATION FOR THE DAY

Keep pouring out yourself to others so that God can keep filling you with His spirit. The more you give, the more you will have for yourself. If you selfishly deny love, the flow from God will cease, and you will again fall into despair. God will see that you are filled as long as you are giving to others.

PRAYER FOR THE DAY

I pray that I may dispel any thought of selfishness. I pray that I may keep the stream of love flowing from God to me to others.

NOVEMBER 3   THOUGHT FOR THE DAY

What comes to us when we finally recognize our incapacity to feel love? We begin to realize that when we become unselfish we will gain the ability to love. Call it faith, call it hope, call it charity, call it "getting the program." What we call it doesn't really matter. From our experience we learn that it comes from a close relationship with a Higher Power. We have experienced it. We have seen it in others. And we will continue to see it in those whose lives are opened to the guidance of the Higher Power. *Have I learned to give and receive love?*

MEDITATION FOR THE DAY

"Ask what you will and it shall be done unto you." God has unlimited power. But we must ask Him for this power, since our indifference to it will block it off. We can go our selfish way without His love, and without the capacity to love. If we have come that path, we know the utter barrenness and futility of the way. How much we gain when we love.

PRAYER FOR THE DAY

I pray that I will keep receiving the strength and capacity to love that I need. I pray that those I meet may acquire from me the same joy.

NOVEMBER 4   THOUGHT FOR THE DAY

I have learned some startling things about myself since I came into this program. Surely one of the most painful was the realization that there is no one in this world whom I can blame for my affliction. My problems lie within me alone, and I am responsible, with the help of the Higher Power, for resolving them. If I can accept this and act upon it, I am on the way to a lasting recovery. *Am I willing to acknowledge that no one else caused my problems and turmoil?*

MEDITATION FOR THE DAY

The attitude so evident during the days of our affliction was one of self-centeredness. It manifested itself in different ways, some of which we now recognize were bitterness, coldness, greed, self-pity, and antagonism toward the Higher Power. Once we made peace with God and began to look to Him for guidance, our whole lives changed. So long as our faith continues, so long as we seek to live in accordance with His will, our lives will be miracles.

PRAYER FOR THE DAY

I pray that I may be given the strength to admit when I am wrong, to acknowledge when I am selfish. I pray that I may accept the responsibility for my recovery.

NOVEMBER 5   THOUGHT FOR THE DAY

When we have been active in the group for a while, we are surprised by some of the things we can do now. We can do things we could not do when we first came into the program. We have found a new kind of peace and contentment. We have found that we are hopeful about the future. We now have real ambition once more, and we can feel charitable toward others. Somewhere along the way we stopped feeling ill. We began to feel new energy, new enthusiasm for living. *Do I fully comprehend how much ground I have already recovered?*

MEDITATION FOR THE DAY

Few of the so-called pleasures in life bring us genuine happiness. If we set about searching selfishly for pleasure for its own sake, happiness will surely elude us. If we follow the guidance of God's spirit and pursue the good, we will experience the contentment and serenity that are true happiness flowing to us in abundant measure.

PRAYER FOR THE DAY

I pray that I may not always seek pleasure as a goal. I pray that happiness may come through doing God's will.

NOVEMBER 6 THOUGHT FOR THE DAY

Now and then many of us still experience fear that threatens to paralyze our efforts. As we continue in this program, we will find ways to control the circumstances that give rise to fear. We come to know what it does to us, how it hinders our growth. We also experience worry. Fear and worry produce tension, which in time can destroy our self-confidence. By putting faith and trust in their place, we drive away fear and worry. *Have I traded my fear and worry for faith and trust?*

MEDITATION FOR THE DAY

In this program we learn to recognize the beauty of the simplest things in life. We are breathing, we are conscious, we awaken to the presence of God. We slowly come alive inside. Our hope is reborn and our faith in God moves us forward each day. We wake to others about us and a world filled with opportunity. Once again we realize that life is for the living—and we are alive.

PRAYER FOR THE DAY

I pray that I may not hamper God's reconstruction of my life. I pray that I may cast out fear and worry.

NOVEMBER 7   THOUGHT FOR THE DAY

We have lost many of our resentments. We have found that getting even with people doesn't do any good. When we try to get revenge, instead of making us feel better, it leaves us frustrated and cheated. We have only hurt our own peace of mind. It does not pay to nurse a grudge. It hurts us more than anyone else. Hatred causes frustration, inner conflict, and affliction. If we give out hate, we will become its victim, for hate only begets more hate. Vengefulness is a powerful poison for us. It separates us from the Higher Power. *Have I lost my resentments?*

MEDITATION FOR THE DAY

It is not you as much as the grace of God within you that helps those around you. If you would help even those you dislike, you have to be certain that there is nothing in you to block the way, to keep God's grace from showing in you. Your own pride and selfishness are blocks. So is hate. Keep those out of the way, and God's grace will flow through you into others.

PRAYER FOR THE DAY

I pray that no hate may flow out from me to others. I pray that I may not harbor feelings that ward others off.

I have lost much of my inferiority complex. I used to bristle when I heard those oblique innuendoes about me. I did not want to face reality. I was constantly steeped in self-pity. I did not recognize the feelings of inadequacy that led me to drift, avoid responsibilities, turn my mind from problems. This program showed me how to get over my feelings of inferiority, helped me want to aspire to something meaningful again. I am a recovering person with a life to reclaim. *Am I convinced that I no longer have time to feel inferior or inadequate?*

MEDITATION FOR THE DAY

We learn to forget what is past, to concentrate on what is ahead. God has forgiven us and asks only that we honestly try to live the way we believe He wants us to live. We have learned to forgive ourselves as well. If we have a genuinely good attitude about ourselves, we can start today with a clean slate and go forward with confidence toward the goal. No goal is too great, so long as we have faith.

PRAYER FOR THE DAY

I pray that I may divest myself of the misery of the past. I pray that today I may start anew with honesty and clarity of vision.

I have learned to be more positive, less negative. I used to take a dim view of almost everything. Most people, I felt, were bluffing. There seemed to be very little good in the world, but a lot of hypocrisy and sham. People could not be trusted. They would use you if they had the chance. Now I am more positive. I believe in people and their capabilities. There are still love, truth, and decency in the world. *Am I more positive and less negative?*

MEDITATION FOR THE DAY

It is not always important to be "right." It is more important to be humane, to be able to show love. When we are these things, we reveal the rightness of God's will.

PRAYER FOR THE DAY

I pray that God may endow me with the important values. I pray that my life may show God's love.

NOVEMBER 10 THOUGHT FOR THE DAY

How can those who have felt the despair of depression describe it to others? They cannot do so until it has been entirely lifted. But we have seen its effects in those who have fallen away from this program and back into the bonds of their affliction. *Am I sure that I want never to endure that kind of depression again?*

MEDITATION FOR THE DAY

When something happens to upset you and you are discouraged, try to feel that life's difficulties and troubles are not intended to arrest your progress in the spiritual life. Think of them as a test of your strength and determination to keep going. Whatever it is that must be met, you are to either overcome it or use it. Nothing should daunt you for long, nor should any difficulty entirely overcome or conquer you. God's strength will always be there, waiting for you to use it.

PRAYER FOR THE DAY

I pray that I may know there will be no failure with God. I pray that my past torment will remain in the past, powerless over me now.

NOVEMBER 11   THOUGHT FOR THE DAY

There are ways in which members tempt fate. Since we are human, we are fallible. To protect ourselves from temptation, we must impose self-restraints on ourselves. Refusing all help will not assure us safety and may greatly aggravate the problem. Such extreme reactions spring from fear, and we must learn to recognize those fears and confront them if we are to maintain rationality. *Do I guard against temptation in rational ways?*

MEDITATION FOR THE DAY

As you look back over your life, it is not too difficult to believe that what you went through was put to a purpose, to prepare you for some valuable work in life. Everything in your life may well be used by God to make you of some particular use in the world. Each person's life is a mosaic of sorts, the pieces ultimately fitting a design of God's preference.

PRAYER FOR THE DAY

I pray that God may have a purpose for my life. I pray that I may be used for some purpose in the world.

NOVEMBER 12   THOUGHT FOR THE DAY

As I look back over the time I have spent in this program, I find that I am far less critical of others now. At first I ran down members of the group because I wanted to build myself up. I was envious of those who lived reasonably normal lives. I couldn't understand why I couldn't be like them. While there surely is hypocrisy and deceit in the world, I've learned now that I can never make a person any better by criticism. *Am I less critical of others?*

MEDITATION FOR THE DAY

You must admit your helplessness before your prayer for help will be heard by God. You must recognize your need before you can ask Him for the strength to meet that need. But once that need is recognized and help is sought, God hears your prayer. You can rest in the certainty that it will be answered, that the strength you need will be forthcoming.

PRAYER FOR THE DAY

I pray that I may be certain that God will hear my prayer. I pray that His strength may come to fill my need.

NOVEMBER 13   THOUGHT FOR THE DAY

Who am I to judge others? Have I proved by my great success in life that I know all the answers? Exactly the opposite. When I came into this program, I had failed in many areas of my life. Am I a fit person to judge others? In this program I have learned not to judge others. Judgment should be left to our Higher Power. *Am I now aware that I must not pass judgment on others?*

MEDITATION FOR THE DAY

Again and again we seem to hear God saying to us, "Come unto Me, all ye that are weary and heavy laden, and I will give you rest." He invites us to come to Him for the solution of every problem, for the overcoming of every temptation, for the calming of every fear, and most of all for the strength to live with peace of mind and the power to be useful and effective.

PRAYER FOR THE DAY

I pray that I may not judge others. I pray that I may go to God for rest and peace of mind.

NOVEMBER 14 THOUGHT FOR THE DAY

Instead of judging others, a better way is to look for all the good in them. If you look hard enough and long enough, you ought to be able to find some good in every person. In this program I learned that my job was to try to bring out the good, not criticize the bad. Every member of this group is used to being criticized and judged. That has never helped anyone recover from his affliction. In this program we tell people they can change. We try to bring out the best in them. We encourage their good points and ignore their bad points. People are not converted by criticism. *Do I look for the good in others?*

MEDITATION FOR THE DAY

There must be a design for the world in the mind of God. We believe that his design for the world is a universal fellowship of men and women under the fathership of God. The plan for your life must also be in the mind of God. In times of quiet meditation you can seek God's guidance, for the revealing of God's plan for your day. Then you can live this day according to that guidance. Many people are not making of their lives what God meant them to be, and so they are unhappy. Those who follow God's guidance are following his design for their lives.

PRAYER FOR THE DAY

I pray that I may try to follow God's design for today. I pray that I may have the sense of Divine Intent in what I do today.

I am less sensitive, and my feelings are less easily hurt. I no longer take myself so seriously. I used to get insulted at the slightest excuse or feel slighted or left out. What happens to me now is not so important. One cause of my problems was that I couldn't take it and tried to find ways to escape unpleasant situations. I have learned not to try to escape or to feel sorry for myself. When I concentrate on this program, I do not notice personal slights so much. They do not seem to matter so much. I have learned to laugh at self-pity because it is childish and dangerous for me. *Am I less sensitive?*

MEDITATION FOR THE DAY

God's miracle-working power is as manifest today as it was in the past. There are still miracles of change in lives and healing of injured minds. When we trust in God and leave it to Him to choose the day and hour, there is God's miracle-working power in our lives, healing our injured minds. We can trust in God and have boundless faith in His power to make us whole again, when he chooses. To want to be healed is itself healing.

PRAYER FOR THE DAY

I pray that I may be certain that there is nothing that God cannot accomplish in changing my life. I pray that I may have faith in His miracle-working power.

I have rid myself of most of my inner conflicts. I was always at war with myself, doing things that I did not want to do. I was on an emotional high one moment and the next moment at the depths of depression and despair. My life was full of broken resolves, frustrated hopes, abandoned plans. I was getting nowhere. This program taught me how to get organized and stop fighting myself. *Have I now rid myself of my inner conflicts?*

MEDITATION FOR THE DAY

"When two or three are gathered together in My name, there am I in the midst of them." The spirit of God comes upon His followers when they are all together at one time, in one place, and with one accord. When two or three consecrated souls are together at a meeting place, the spirit of God is there to help and guide them. Where any sincere group of people are together, reverently seeking the help of God, His power and His spirit are there to inspire them.

PRAYER FOR THE DAY

I pray that I may be in accord with those who gather together. I pray that I may feel the strength of a consecrated group.

Everyone tends to have two personalities. We are all dual to some extent. When we were in turmoil, the selfish, resentful, jealous, self-pitying side of our personality took over our lives. When we were rational, we were different people. But then once again turmoil would bring out the worst in us. So we were always divided, always in conflict with our other selves. In this program, we began to pull ourselves together, to become unified, to stop battling and give ourselves wholeheartedly to this program and to rationality. *Do I now have a more unified, rational personality?*

MEDITATION FOR THE DAY

"Well done, thou good and faithful servant. Enter into the joy of Thy Lord." These words are for many ordinary people whom the world may pass by, unrecognizing. Not to the world-famed, the proud, the wealthy are these words spoken, but to the quiet followers who serve God unobtrusively yet faithfully, who bear their crosses bravely and show a smiling face to the world. "Enter into the joy of Thy Lord." Pass into that fuller spiritual life, which is a life of joy and peace.

PRAYER FOR THE DAY

I pray that I may not desire the world's applause. I pray that I may not seek rewards for doing what I believe is right.

NOVEMBER 18   THOUGHT FOR THE DAY

The procrastinator's motto is, "Don't put off till to-morrow what you can put off till next week." We often put off action because we are afraid of making a mistake. The thought of action can all but paralyze us or send us into a panic. We can dwell on the problem, finding seemingly rational reasons for inaction until we lose all sense of proportion. We need someone to turn to who can help us make sense of our problem. That is why we advise each of our members to have a sponsor — someone to turn to for advice and willing support — someone who will make sense of our non-sense and encourage us to take action. *Do I support the sponsorship activity of this group?*

MEDITATION FOR THE DAY

Raise your thoughts from the mundane, the sordid, the casual concerns of the worldly life. Look to the heights of decency, of beauty, of devotion to the needs of others. The glory of God will be reflected in your character. The glory of God is too dazzling for mortals to see fully on this earth. But some of His glory is glimpsed in you when you try to reflect that light in your life.

PRAYER FOR THE DAY

I pray that I may look up to the heights. I pray that some of the Divine Light may be reflected in my life.

Putting sex in its proper place is one of the rewards that come to us in this program. We now subject each relationship to the test: Is it selfish? Is it hurtful to another? Moral, unselfish living ensures that our lives are free of overindulgence and guilt. We can ask God to mold our ideals and help us to live up to them. We can act accordingly. *Do I exercise moderation and unselfishness in my sexual relationships?*

MEDITATION FOR THE DAY

"I will lift up my eyes unto the heights whence cometh my help." Try to raise your thoughts from the depths of the sordid and mean and impure things of the earth to the heights of goodness and decency and beauty. Train your insight by trying to take the higher view. Train it more and more until distant heights become more familiar. The heights of God, whence cometh your help, will become nearer and dearer, and the false values of the earth will seem farther away.

PRAYER FOR THE DAY

I pray that I may not keep my eyes forever downcast. I pray that I may set my sights on higher things.

NOVEMBER 20   THOUGHT FOR THE DAY

I no longer try to escape life through the crutches of alcohol, drugs, food, emotionalism, or any other compulsion. In my affliction I built an unreal world. Each bout with turmoil made it harder to face the reality of life. The more I tried to escape the more my personality weakened. One escape after another drove out calm and reason, control and sanity. Now I see that the life I was living was a nightmare. This program taught me not to run away but to face reality. *Have I given up trying to escape life?*

MEDITATION FOR THE DAY

In these times of quiet meditation try more and more to set your hopes on the grace of God. Know that, whatever the future may hold, it will hold more and more of good. Do not set all your hopes and desires on material things. There is weariness in an abundance of things. Set your hopes on spiritual things so that you may grow spiritually. Learn to rely on God's power more and more, and in that reliance you will have an insight into the greater value of the things of the spirit.

PRAYER FOR THE DAY

I pray that I may not be overwhelmed by material things. I pray that I may realize the higher value of spiritual things.

Part of my turmoil revolved around money. I wasted money on foolish things. Spending lavishly gave me a feeling of comfort, a sense of importance. Now that I am recovering, I spend my hard-earned money as it should be spent. I do not throw it away. I give to this program so that it will help pay its way and to assure that it will always be here for others who need it as I need it. *Am I making good use of my money?*

MEDITATION FOR THE DAY

You were meant to be at home and comfortable in the world. Yet some people live a life of quiet desperation. This is the opposite of being at home and at peace in the world. Let your peace of mind be evident to those around you. Let others see that you are comfortable and, seeing it, know that it springs from your trust in a Higher Power. The dull, hard way of resignation is not God's way. Faith takes the sting out of the winds of adversity and brings peace even in the midst of struggle.

PRAYER FOR THE DAY

I pray that I may be more responsible in my way of living. I pray that I may feel more at home and at peace within myself.

I have rid myself of my restlessness. When I came into this program, I felt a kind of restlessness. I could not understand how others about me could be so calm and serene while I was churning inside. But as a new life opened for me, I gave this program time and enthusiasm. And soon I did not have time to be restless or bored. *Have I rid myself of the fear of becoming restless or bored?*

MEDITATION FOR THE DAY

To have charity means to care enough about your fellow man to want to do something for him. A smile, a word of encouragement, a word of love goes on its way, simple though it may seem, while the mighty words of an orator fall on deaf ears. Use up the odd moments of your day trying to do something to help another. Restlessness, like boredom, comes from thinking too much about yourself.

PRAYER FOR THE DAY

I pray that I may try to overcome the self-centeredness that makes me restless and bored. I pray that I may do some act of charity for another.

NOVEMBER 23 THOUGHT FOR THE DAY

I no longer refuse to do anything because I cannot do it to perfection. Many of us used the excuse of not being able to do something perfectly to enable us to do nothing at all. We pretended to be perfectionists. We were experts at telling others how a thing should be done, but we balked when it came to doing it ourselves. We said to ourselves that we might make a mistake and so it was better not to attempt it. Now we know that this illogic can lead us right back to our former turmoil, where mistakes reigned supreme. We know that the mere fact that we can never achieve perfection does not prevent us from doing the best we can. *Have I stopped hiding behind the screen of perfectionism?*

MEDITATION FOR THE DAY

"Be of good cheer. I have overcome the world." Just as surely as He came to free the world, you can rise above the world's turmoil into the secret place of perfect peace and confidence. When a challenge comes to you, remember that you have the power of God to help you. With God's help, nothing can wholly defeat you.

PRAYER FOR THE DAY

I pray that I may not fear the threat of failure. I pray that I may have confidence and be of good cheer.

Instead of being perfectionists, in this program we are content if we are making progress. The main thing is to be growing. We realize that perfectionism is a result of false pride and an excuse to save face. In this program we are willing to make mistakes and to stumble, provided we are always stumbling forward. We are not so interested in what we are as in what we are becoming. We are on the way, not at the goal. And we will be on the way as long as we live. None of us has achieved perfection. But we are getting better. *Am I making forward progress?*

MEDITATION FOR THE DAY

Each new day brings an opportunity to do some little thing that will help to make a better world, bringing God's kingdom a little nearer to realization on earth. Take each day's events as opportunities to do something for God. You can offer the day's service to God, which gives you a share in His work. You do not have to do great things.

PRAYER FOR THE DAY

I pray that today I may do the next thing, the unselfish thing, the loving thing. I pray that I may be content with doing small things for God.

This program teaches me to curb envy and jealousy of others' capacities or possessions. Before I came into this program, I envied those who lived normal lives. I was jealous of their poise, their calmness, their self-confidence. I envied them their material possessions. Now I don't have to be envious any more. I try not to want what I don't deserve. I am content with what I have earned by my efforts to live the right way. *Am I rid of the corrosive feeling of envy?*

MEDITATION FOR THE DAY

Gratitude to God is the theme of the Thanksgiving season. The Pilgrims gathered to give thanks to God for their harvest. When you survey your harvest of peace and serenity, you give thanks to God. In the quiet moments of thanksgiving, you sense the spirit of God entering and filling your being.

PRAYER FOR THE DAY

I pray that my days may be filled with thanksgiving. I pray that the spirit of God may fill my being.

NOVEMBER 26   THOUGHT FOR THE DAY

We have been thinking about some of the rewards that have come to us as a result of our new way of living. We have found that we have rid ourselves of many of our fears, resentments, feelings of inferiority, negative points of view, self-centeredness, criticism of others, oversensitiveness, inner conflicts, procrastination, undisciplined sex, waste of money, restlessness, boredom, perfectionism, and jealousy and envy of others. We are thankful to be rid of our turmoil, and we are also thankful to be rid of these other things. We can now go forward in the new way of life, as shown us by this program. *Am I ready to go forward in the new life?*

MEDITATION FOR THE DAY

"He that has eyes to see, let him see." To the seeing eye, the world is good. Pray for a seeing eye, to see the purpose of God in everything good. Pray for enough faith to see God's care in His dealings with you. Try to see how He has brought you safely through your past life so that now you can be of use in the world. With the eyes of faith you can see God's care and purpose everywhere.

PRAYER FOR THE DAY

I pray that I may have a seeing eye. I pray that with the eye of faith I may see God's purpose everywhere

NOVEMBER 27   THOUGHT FOR THE DAY

The way of this program is the way of rationality, fellowship, service, and faith. Let us take up each one of these and see if our feet are truly on the path. The first is rationality. The others are built upon it as the foundation. We could not have the others if we did not have rationality. We came into this program to regain our sanity, and we work to help others recover. We cannot build any decent kind of life unless we stay rational. *Am I now rational?*

MEDITATION FOR THE DAY

Truly to desire to do God's will—therein lies happiness. We begin by wanting our own way. We want our wills to be satisfied. We take and we do not give. Gradually we find that we are not happy when we are selfish, and so we begin to make allowances for the wills of others. But we begin to be truly happy when we try to do God's will. We learn God's will for us in these quiet times of meditation.

PRAYER FOR THE DAY

I pray that I may subordinate my will to the will of God. I pray that I may be guided today to find His will for me.

NOVEMBER 28   THOUGHT FOR THE DAY

This program is the way of rationality. It is a program that has been successful with many afflictions. Doctors, psychiatrists, and clergymen have had some success. Some men and women have recovered by themselves. We believe that this program is the most successful and the happiest way to recovery for us. Some are unable to achieve success and backslide into turmoil after some degree of recovery. But they too may recover if they return to the program. *Am I deeply grateful to have found this program?*

MEDITATION FOR THE DAY

What sort of rest is satisfying rest? Is it a physical condition, an emotional or mental state? In quiet moments of meditation we reflect on our new way of living, we seek to discern what God's will is for our lives, and we surrender our lives to His will. Then do we find peace and satisfying rest.

PRAYER FOR THE DAY

I pray that I may seek to follow the will of God. I pray that in doing His will I may find rest.

NOVEMBER 29   THOUGHT FOR THE DAY

This program is the way of rationality, and yet there are failures. Why do they occur? Why don't all of us accept the principles of the program and stay rational? There are many reasons, but it has been proved that there is no cure for our affliction. It can only be arrested. Many have tried to return to the old ways of living, the old distorted thinking, and the results have generally been disastrous. *Am I convinced that the old ways of living are not for me?*

MEDITATION FOR THE DAY

Abiding faith is attainable by each of us. To acquire faith is to be open with God. God will accept any form of communication we offer, as long as it is genuine. When we are in need of God's help, our communion with Him assures us that His help will come.

PRAYER FOR THE DAY

I pray that I may attain abiding faith. I pray that I may rest in the assurance of His help in time of need.

There is backsliding in our program. It has been said that these are not accidents but premeditated reversions to old ways of living. We usually have thought about it before it happened. The thought precedes the action. Here is where fellowship comes in. One who is tempted is encouraged to get in touch with another member before doing anything. There is an excellent chance that the whole disastrous experience can be avoided. Members who see someone in danger of backsliding can make contact and try to get the person back on the path. *Am I on my guard against dangerous thinking?*

MEDITATION FOR THE DAY

You can get away from the misunderstanding of others by retiring into your own place of meditation. But from yourself, from your sense of failure, your weakness, your guilt feelings, there is no escape. The only way is to strengthen your faith as you sense it weakening. Ask God to strengthen you. As His spirit envelops you, your weakness is lost in His strength, and you become in harmony with Him again.

PRAYER FOR THE DAY

I pray that I may lose my weakness in the strength of God's spirit. I pray that I may trust Him to keep me on the path.

DECEMBER 1   THOUGHT FOR THE DAY

The thoughts that come before backsliding are often subconscious. It is a question whether or not our subconscious minds ever become entirely free from irrational ideas as long as we live. As we sleep, some of us dream about the past turmoil long after we come into this program. But in offering service to others, we have a means whereby we can divest ourselves, even subconsciously in time, of the danger of backsliding. To give service is to put ourselves into positive action that benefits us as well. *Do I realize that giving service to others helps me?*

MEDITATION FOR THE DAY

Have sympathy and compassion for all who are in temptation. It is a condition we are sometimes in, and we have a responsibility toward them. Sympathy always includes responsibility. Pity is useless, for it does not have a remedy for the need. Wherever our sympathy goes, our responsibility goes. When we are moved with compassion, we should go to those in need and be a channel of God's power to them.

PRAYER FOR THE DAY

I pray that I will not be troubled by thoughts of the past. I pray that I may have compassion for others in temptation.

The unconscious thoughts precede backsliding; but at least a part of those thoughts gets into the conscious mind. An idle thought about the past casually pops into mind. That is a critical moment. If we use faith to ward off the effects of that disruptive thinking, we have realized yet another role in which our Higher Power offers us help. Left unchallenged, that critical moment can lead to disaster. We must summon faith. Then we must seek help. *Do I summon faith when critical moments come?*

MEDITATION FOR THE DAY

Many of us have a vision of the kind of person God wants us to be. We must be true to that vision, whatever it is, and we must try to live up to it. We can also believe that God has a vision of what He wants us to be. In all people there is the person that God sees in us and wills us to be. With His help we can strive toward His vision of us.

PRAYER FOR THE DAY

I pray that I may strive to be the kind of person that God would have me be. I pray that I may fulfill His vision of what I could be.

DECEMBER 3   THOUGHT FOR THE DAY

There is some distorted thinking, conscious or unconscious, that comes before every backsliding. As long as we live, we must be on the lookout for such thinking and guard against it. In fact, our training in this program is mostly to prepare us to recognize such thoughts and reject them at once. Backsliding occurs when we allow such thinking to remain in our minds. This program is one of mental training. *How well is my mind prepared to handle distorted thoughts?*

MEDITATION FOR THE DAY

Do not trouble your mind with puzzles you cannot solve. The solutions may never be shown to you until you have left this life The inequities, injuries, tragedies are beyond your understanding. Only step by step, stage by stage, can you proceed on your journey into greater knowledge and deeper understanding.

PRAYER FOR THE DAY

I pray that I may not worry about things I do not now understand. I pray that I may have faith that someday I may have deeper understanding.

DECEMBER 4   THOUGHT FOR THE DAY

If we allow a distorted thought to lodge in our minds, we are in danger of reverting to past ways. Therefore, we must dispel such thoughts at once by putting constructive thoughts in their place. We remember that the turmoil of the past is disastrous for us. We remember that one step backward can lead to misery and defeat. Determine not to take the risk. Fill your mind with constructive thoughts. Concentrate on the peace of your newfound rationality. *Am I keeping my thoughts constructive?*

MEDITATION FOR THE DAY

Always seek to set aside the values of the world that seem wrong and try to judge only by those values that seem right to you. Do not seek the praise and notice of others. Be one who, though sometimes scoffed at, has the serenity and peace of mind that they may never know.

PRAYER FOR THE DAY

I pray that I may not heed too much the judgment of others. I pray that I may judge by the values that are right and true.

DECEMBER 5   THOUGHT FOR THE DAY

In spite of all we have learned in this program, our old way of thinking comes back to us, sometimes with overwhelming force. Sometimes it is because we forget to call on our Higher Power for assurance. Sometimes we seem to make our minds a blank, forget our training, and revert to our past way of thinking. Our service to others does not guarantee our own immunity from temptation, but it certainly affords one of the best assurances against letting things get out of hand. We learned to get this program by giving it away. *Am I convinced that I will never become complacent or neglect my training?*

MEDITATION FOR THE DAY

Give something to those with problems. Give them your sympathy, your prayers, your time, your love, your thought, your self. Then give of your own confidence as it was given to you by the grace of God. They are in need as you once were in need. Give your best to those who need it and will accept it.

PRAYER FOR THE DAY

I pray that, as I have received from others, so may I give to others. I pray that the answer I give may be the one that they need.

DECEMBER 6   THOUGHT FOR THE DAY

In responding to a Twelfth Step call from someone who has slipped, you instantly sense the person's discomfort and shame. Some feel such shame that they do not want to return to the program. They feel that they are worthless, hopeless, unable to make it. They feel worse off than before. But even then their past experience can help. They must be convinced that coming back is essential, that the help of the Higher Power is theirs for the asking. *Do I realize that I can never lose entirely what this program has taught me?*

MEDITATION FOR THE DAY

No one entirely escapes temptation. You must expect it and be ready for it when it comes. None of us is entirely safe. You must be able to recognize temptation when it comes. The first step toward conquering it always is to see it clearly as temptation and refuse to harbor it in your mind. Call upon the Higher Power for help. Daily thought and prayer will help you keep up your defenses. Group meetings will bolster you. Meditations such as this will strengthen you, for here you reach for the power of God.

PRAYER FOR THE DAY

I pray that I may be prepared for whatever temptation may come to me. I pray that I may see it clearly and summon the help of God.

DECEMBER 7   THOUGHT FOR THE DAY

This program requires personal honesty. To be honest is often difficult. But it is essential if we are to overcome habits of thought that lead back to turmoil. No one forces us to be honest. It is left to us entirely. Failure to do so will have no effect on the group's capacity for honesty. Only the person who evades the challenge endures the consequences. If backsliding is the issue, guilt makes honesty even more difficult. Having discussed it with the group, the person regains confidence and is at ease again. *Am I understanding of others' mistakes?*

MEDITATION FOR THE DAY

We form an alliance with God to gain strength, to begin a new life and to gain spiritual power. We do so for we have learned that we cannot otherwise sustain life in any meaningful way. The old life, the turmoil that brought us here, is gone. With the spirit of God within us, we are refreshed and renewed.

PRAYER FOR THE DAY

I pray that I may do the will of God. I pray that I may gain new spiritual power from Him for the new life ahead.

DECEMBER 8   THOUGHT FOR THE DAY

The length of time of our rationality is not as important as the quality of it. Some members who have been around for a long time may not yet have achieved serenity or peace. There is great satisfaction to have been in the program for a long time, but even older members must guard against backsliding. We can learn from them, but we must remember that the quality of the new life is more important than how long we have lived it. *What is the quality of my rationality?*

MEDITATION FOR THE DAY

We can do greater things when we have more experience in the new way of life. Opportunities for a better life are all around us. But we do not work alone, nor is any of it possible without the help, guidance, and blessing of the Higher Power. As we give, we will receive. As we learn, so will we teach. Our example is as instructive as our words.

PRAYER FOR THE DAY

I pray that I may find my rightful place in the world. I pray that the quality of my new life may be sustained by the grace of God.

DECEMBER 9   THOUGHT FOR THE DAY

"No man is an island." No one is intended to live alone. All of us need to be by ourselves sometimes, but we cannot live without the fellowship of others. Our natures demand it. Our lives depend largely upon it. What we find in this program is a mutual exchange of trust, faith, and understanding. *Do I fully appreciate what the fellowship of this program means to me?*

MEDITATION FOR THE DAY

We are all seeking something, but many do not know what it is. They are seeking because they are restless and dissatisfied. They do not yet realize that faith in God can give them a meaning in life. If you have found a Higher Power, you can be the means of leading others, showing them that their search for a meaning in life will end when they find faith and trust in God.

PRAYER FOR THE DAY

I pray that I may have tranquillity in the knowledge that I have found a meaning in life. I pray that I may lead others to faith and trust in God.

DECEMBER 10 THOUGHT FOR THE DAY

We had some degree of fellowship in the company we kept before we came into this program. We spent many hours with them and felt they were our friends. Now we discover that we never see any of them, now that we no longer are in turmoil. Some of us were loners, and for us the fellowship of this program is a new and rewarding experience. Now we know what real friendship is. Our former friendships were only misery looking for company. *Do I see past friendships in their real light?*

MEDITATION FOR THE DAY

Set for yourself the task of growing daily more and more into the consciousness of a Higher Power. We must keep trying to improve our conscious contact with God. This is done by prayer, quiet times, and communion. Often all you need to do is sit silent before God and let Him speak to you through your thought. Try to think God's thoughts after Him. When the guidance comes, you must not hesitate, but go out and follow that guidance in your daily work, doing what you believe to be the right thing.

PRAYER FOR THE DAY

I pray that I may be still and know that God is with me. I pray that I may open my mind to the leading of the Divine Mind.

DECEMBER 11 THOUGHT FOR THE DAY

Many think of this program as group therapy. In some ways that is true, but that is only part of it. To look at it only as a means of staying rational is a selfish view. The fellowship of this program has far greater significance beyond personal benefit. There is the spiritual realm as well, and it is here that the program far exceeds the goals of group therapy. So often that is the reason it succeeds where group therapy fails. *Do I now deeply feel the true fellowship of this program?*

MEDITATION FOR THE DAY

Most of us have had to live through the dark part of our lives, the time of failure, the nighttime of our lives, when we were full of struggle and care, worry and remorse, when we felt deeply the tragedy of life. But with our daily surrender to a Higher Power come a peace and joy that make all things new. We can now take each day as a joyous sunrise-gift from God, to use for Him and for other people. The night of the past is gone; this day is ours.

PRAYER FOR THE DAY

I pray that I may take this day as a gift from God. I pray that I may thank God for this day and be glad in it.

DECEMBER 12   THOUGHT FOR THE DAY

The spiritual fellowship of this program is more like the fellowship of the church than mere group therapy. It is based on a common belief in God and a common effort to live a better spiritual life. The program encourages this, and also its members help each other cope with the personal problems in their lives. By being open we are of service to one another, for we share our own experiences that others may find answers to their needs. *Do I appreciate the deep personal nature of this program's fellowship?*

MEDITATION FOR THE DAY

Love and fear cannot dwell together. By their very natures they cannot exist side by side. Fear is a very strong force. A weak and vacillating love can soon be destroyed by fear. But a strong love that is based on trust in God is eventually able to conquer fear. Fear is dispelled by having love of God in one's heart.

PRAYER FOR THE DAY

I pray that love will drive fear and anguish from my life. I pray that others can know the peace that love brings.

DECEMBER 13   THOUGHT FOR THE DAY

Our fellowship is partly group therapy. It is partly spiritual fellowship. But it is even more. We share a common affliction in our group. This is a highly personal fellowship in which our innermost thoughts and problems are shared. We sweep aside all barriers to help each other get well. We can be sure of sympathy, understanding, and real compassion. *Do I fully appreciate the depth of this fellowship?*

MEDITATION FOR THE DAY

In our efforts to recover we have sought divine guidance. We have tried to adopt a different attitude toward ourselves. Just as God in His endless patience repeatedly offers forgiveness to us, now we are learning to forgive ourselves for the mistakes we have made. And we forgive others, as God forgives us.

PRAYER FOR THE DAY

I pray that I may choose the right. I pray that I may forgive others as I am forgiven.

DECEMBER 14   THOUGHT FOR THE DAY

The way of this program is the way of service. Without that, it would not work. We have been without our turmoil and hated it. We have made a commitment and impatiently waited for the time of our trial to end. We have tried all manner of relief, but until we begin to help others we do not experience full satisfaction in our rationality. In this program we receive, and then we give what we have received. We cannot hold back without losing what we received. *Have I given up all ideas of holding this program for myself alone?*

MEDITATION FOR THE DAY

Try to see the life of the spirit as a calm place, shut away from the tumult of the world. Think of your spiritual home as a place filled with peace, serenity, and contentment. Go to this place to meditate and gain the strength to carry you through the day's problems. Go back daily and whenever you are weary of the world.

PRAYER FOR THE DAY

I pray that I may keep this resting place where I can commune with God. I pray that there I may find rest and understanding.

Service to others makes the world a better place. Civilization would cease if all of us were always and only for ourselves. We have a wonderful opportunity to contribute to the well-being of the world. We have a common problem, and we find a common answer. We are uniquely equipped to help others with the same problem. What a wonderful world it would be if everybody took his own greatest problem, found an answer, and then shared it with others like himself. There would soon be the right kind of world. *Do I appreciate my unique opportunities to be of service?*

MEDITATION FOR THE DAY

Today can be lived in conscious contact with God, who is upholding you in all good words, thoughts, and deeds. When a shadow descends on your life, it is not the withdrawal of God's presence but only your own temporary fear and unrest. The dull gray days are for doing what you must do. Your Higher Power is there every day, whenever you seek Him.

PRAYER FOR THE DAY

I pray that I may face the dull gray days with courage. I pray that I may have the faith that the bright days will return.

DECEMBER 16 THOUGHT FOR THE DAY

Faith is imperative in this program. We do not gain the full benefit of it until we surrender our lives to a Power greater than ourselves. We also trust that Power to give us the strength we need. There is no better way for us. We can be rational without it, but if we are going to truly live without fear, we must have faith. That is our path, and we must follow it. *Have I taken the way of faith?*

MEDITATION FOR THE DAY

Life is not a search for happiness. Happiness is a by-product of living the right way, of doing the right thing. Search not for happiness but for right living. Then happiness will be your reward. Life is sometimes a burden of duty and commitments. But happiness will come again, as God's smile of recognition of your faithfulness. True happiness is always the by-product of a life well lived.

PRAYER FOR THE DAY

I pray that I may not seek happiness but seek to do right. I pray that I may not seek pleasure but seek that which will bring happiness.

The way of faith is not, of course, confined to this program. It is the way for everyone who wants to really live. But many people go through life without much faith. Many are doing so, to their own sorrow. The world is bleak from lack of faith, and many have lost confidence in any meaning in the universe. But for us the way of faith is the way of life. We have proved by our past lives that we could not live without it. *Do I think I could live without faith now?*

MEDITATION FOR THE DAY

The Higher Power does not interfere with the working of natural laws. It rains alike on rich and poor, on just and unjust. Natural laws are unchanging, and spiritual laws are made to be obeyed. On our choice of good or evil do we rise or fall, experience victory or defeat. We have known defeat, and now we are learning the joy of victory.

PRAYER FOR THE DAY

I pray that I may choose today the way of the spiritual life. I pray that I may live today with hope and faith.

DECEMBER 18 THOUGHT FOR THE DAY

Unless we have the key of faith to unlock the meaning of life, we are lost. We choose faith not because it is one way for us but because it is the only way. Many have failed and will fail again. For others there is no life of victory without faith. We are at sea without a rudder, aimlessly drifting, when we attempt to live without faith. Life is a meaningless succession of the kinds of turmoil we had in the past. *Do I realize that faith is imperative to my recovery?*

MEDITATION FOR THE DAY

It is in the moment of testing that we come to know our inner strength. There is no way to know what we will do at that moment of truth. Some of us have survived these moments. Some have fallen before them. There is no preparation but to find faith in a Higher Power and to serve others in their need.

PRAYER FOR THE DAY

I pray that I may not worry about the limitation of my human mind. I pray that my faith will help me meet any moment of test.

DECEMBER 19   THOUGHT FOR THE DAY

All around us are the skeptics, the agnostics. There is also the world of the believers, of the losers given another chance. Which we choose to see helps determine how we regard life. The wrongs are there, but the truths are there, too. We are surely on the right path when we choose a life of hope through faith. *Have I chosen the path of faith?*

MEDITATION FOR THE DAY

We may compare the material world with the clay that the artist works with. Is it molded into something beautiful or something ugly? Like the artist we can mold the clay of our lives into something beautiful or something ugly. We can mold something beautiful — love and good will—out of our lives.

PRAYER FOR THE DAY

I pray that I may make something good out of my life. I pray that I may be a good artisan of the clay of my life.

DECEMBER 20   THOUGHT FOR THE DAY

Our faith should control the whole of our lives. We were living a divided life and had to find a way to make it whole. When we were irrational, our lives were made up of scattered and unrelated pieces. Now we are picking up the parts and putting them together again. We do it with faith, which binds us together. This gives us all the meaning and purpose we require. *Am I becoming whole again?*

MEDITATION FOR THE DAY

Avoid fear as you would a plague. Fear is a hacking at the cords of faith that bind you to your Higher Power. However small the fraying, in time those cords will wear thin, and one disappointment or shock could break them. Avoid the self-indulgence of self-pity and depression, which allow fear to gain a hold. Fear is the denial of God's care and protection.

PRAYER FOR THE DAY

I pray that I may have such trust in God today that I will not fear anything. I pray that I may trust in God's loving care.

DECEMBER 21   THOUGHT FOR THE DAY

Have I ceased to be inwardly defeated and at war with myself? Have I given myself freely to this program and to the Higher Power? Have I stopped wandering and begun collecting my wits? I believe now that I can face anything, if I am sure that I am on the way. When I am sure, I should bet my life on it. That is how I understand the program works. I will follow it to the best of my ability, as I know I must. *Am I going to let these principles guide me in life?*

MEDITATION FOR THE DAY

In this time of quiet meditation follow the pressure of God's leading. In all decisions to be made today, yield to the gentle urging of your conscience. Stay or go as that pressure indicates. Take the events of today as a part of God's planning and ordering of your life. He will lead you to a right decision.

PRAYER FOR THE DAY

I pray that today I may try to follow the pressure of God's leading. I pray that I may try to follow my conscience and do what seems right today.

DECEMBER 22 THOUGHT FOR THE DAY

As we look back over our lives of affliction, we must realize that they were a mess because we were a mess inside. The biggest trouble was in us, not in life itself. Life itself was good enough, but we were looking at it the wrong way. We were looking at life through sick, distorted concepts, and naturally it was distorted, too. We could not see the beauty, the goodness, and the purpose in the world. Others saw us as we were, but we could not see ourselves clearly. *Can I now see life and myself as they are?*

MEDITATION FOR THE DAY

Fear no evil, because the power of God can conquer evil. Evil has power to seriously hurt only those who do not place themselves under the protection of a Higher Power. This is not a question of feeling but an assured fact of our experience. We trust in God as our defense. Let even the hope of something we desire be used, if necessary, to intensify our trust.

PRAYER FOR THE DAY

I pray that fear will not overtake me. I pray that I may try to place myself under the protection of God's grace.

We have definitely left the dream world of our affliction behind. It was a sham. It was a world of our own
making, not the real world. We are sorry for the past,
yes; but we learned a lot from it. We can put it down
to experience, because it has given us insight about
the ways that won't work. It gave us knowledge that
we needed to make us face reality. Through our misery we finally came into this program. *Do I look upon
my errors of the past as valuable experience?*

MEDITATION FOR THE DAY

Dispense peace, not discord. Try to be part of the cure
of every situation, not part of the malady. Try to ignore evil rather than actively combat it. Always try to
build up, never to tear down. Show others by your
example that happiness comes from living the right
way. The power of your example is greater than the
power of what you say.

PRAYER FOR THE DAY

I pray that I may try to bring something good into
every situation today. I pray that I may be constructive in living today.

We have been given a new life, just because we were afflicted. We certainly don't deserve the new life that has been given us. There is little in our past to warrant the life we have now. Many people live good lives from their youth onward, not getting into serious conflicts. We are among the lucky few who have learned a new way to live. *Am I deeply grateful for the new life I have begun through this program?*

MEDITATION FOR THE DAY

We have a deep gratitude to the Higher Power for all the blessings that we have and that we don't seem to deserve. We thank Him and mean it. We now give service to others, out of gratitude for what we have received. We make some sacrifices to do so, but we are glad to do it. Gratitude, service, and sacrifice are the steps up to the door to a new life.

PRAYER FOR THE DAY

I pray that I may gladly serve others out of deep gratitude for what I have received. I pray that I may keep a deep sense of obligation.

DECEMBER 25   THOUGHT FOR THE DAY

Most of us will say today, "This is a good Christmas."
They will be looking back over past Christmases that
were not like this one at all. They will be thanking
God for their recovery and their new life. They will be
thinking about how their lives were changed when
they came into this program. They will be thinking
that perhaps God let them live when they were close
to death in order that they might be used by Him,
later on. *Is this a happier Christmas for me?*

MEDITATION FOR THE DAY

The kingdom of heaven is also for the lowly, the sinners, the repentant. "And they presented unto him
gifts—gold, frankincense, and myrrh." Bring your
gifts of gold—your money and material possessions.
Bring your frankincense—the consecration of your
life to a worthy cause. Bring your myrrh—your
sympathy and understanding and help. Lay them all
at the feet of God and let Him have full use of them.

PRAYER FOR THE DAY

I pray that I may be truly thankful on this Christmas
Day. I pray that I may bring my gifts and lay them on
the altar.

I am glad to be a part of this program, of this great and growing fellowship. I am only one of many members, but I am one. I am grateful to be living at this time when I can help the program grow and when I am needed to help keep the movement going. I am useful and have a reason for living. I also now have a purpose in life, to devote myself to this great effort. *Am I truly aware how many ways I can be thankful?*

MEDITATION FOR THE DAY

Meditation can teach us how to relax. We can be helpful in a small way, sometimes just by being relaxed. We should not worry too much about those we cannot help. We can make it a habit to leave the outcome to God. It is to our benefit, sometimes, that we go back and reconsider some of what we have read through the year. We will see much more clearly God's role in our recovery.

PRAYER FOR THE DAY

I pray that I may give myself to this worthwhile cause in any way I can. I pray that I may enjoy the satisfaction that comes from working with others.

DECEMBER 27   THOUGHT FOR THE DAY

In all ways I need the principles of this program for the development of the buried life within me. It is a good life that I misplaced but I found again in this fellowship. This life within me is developing slowly but surely, even with setbacks, mistakes, failures. As long as I stay in the program, my life will go on developing. I cannot yet know what it will be, but I know that it will be better by far than what it was. *Am I thanking God for this program?*

MEDITATION FOR THE DAY

Build your life on the firm foundation of true gratitude to God for all His blessings and help. Build the frame of your life out of self-discipline, never selfishness. Build the walls of service, the roof of prayer and God's guidance. Build a garden around your life of peace and serenity. Occupy your house with love.

PRAYER FOR THE DAY

I pray that I may build my life well. I pray that it may be a good building when my work is finished.

DECEMBER 28   THOUGHT FOR THE DAY

This program is human in its organization, but it is divine in its purpose. The purpose is to point me toward a God of my understanding and the good life. My feet have been set upon the right path. I am going in the right direction. I feel it in the depths of my being. Whatever the future holds, it cannot be too much for me to bear. I have a Divine Power with me to carry me through everything I may encounter. *Am I pointed in the right direction for the good life?*

MEDITATION FOR THE DAY

Although unseen, the Lord is always near to those who believe in Him and trust and depend on Him for strength. Veiled from mortal sight, the Higher Power is always available if we but ask. The feeling that God is with us never leaves regardless of momentary distractions. We are conscious of His power and use His protection as a shield.

PRAYER FOR THE DAY

I pray that today I may feel that God is not too far away to depend on for help. I pray that I may feel confident of His readiness to give me the power that I need.

DECEMBER 29   THOUGHT FOR THE DAY

Since I participate in the privileges of the group, I will share the responsibilities, taking it upon myself to carry my fair share of the load, not grudgingly but joyfully. I am deeply grateful for membership privileges. They put an obligation upon me that I will not evade. Because of the joy of sharing the burdens, they become opportunities. *Will I accept each opportunity gladly?*

MEDITATION FOR THE DAY

Work and prayer are the two forces that are gradually making a better world. We must work for the betterment of ourselves and others. Faith without works is dead. But all work with people should be based on prayer. If we say a prayer before we try to help, it will make us more effective. Nothing is impossible in human relationships if we depend upon the help of God.

PRAYER FOR THE DAY

I pray that my life may be balanced between prayer and work. I pray that I may carry on with faith, with prayer, and with hope.

DECEMBER 30   THOUGHT FOR THE DAY

To the extent that I fail in my responsibilities, the program fails. To the extent that I succeed, the program succeeds. Every failure of mine will set back the work to that extent. Every success of mine will put it ahead to that extent. I shall not wait to be selected for service but will volunteer. I shall accept each opportunity to work for the program as another challenge. *Have I been willing to meet these challenges so far?*

MEDITATION FOR THE DAY

People are failures in the deepest sense when they seek to live without God's sustaining power. Many try to be self-sufficient and seek selfish pleasure and find that it does not work too well. No matter how much fame and material wealth they acquire, the time of disillusionment and futility comes. Death is ahead, and they cannot take any material thing with them. One may gain the world and have nothing.

PRAYER FOR THE DAY

I pray that I will not come to the end of life empty and barren of spirit. I pray that I may so live that I will not be afraid to die.

DECEMBER 31   THOUGHT FOR THE DAY

I shall be loyal in my attendance, generous in my giving, kind in my criticism, creative in my suggestions, and loving in my attitudes. I shall give this program my interest, my enthusiasm, my devotion, and myself. The Lord's Prayer is vital in our meetings and also in my everyday life. I need to recall its words each day and on this Eve rededicate myself to the promise that I made. Let it be my guiding influence another year. *Am I satisfied that I have tried steadily through the year to make the program work for me?*

MEDITATION FOR THE DAY

As we look back over the year, it has been a good year. It is good to the extent that we have put good efforts, good words, and good thoughts into it. None need be wasted. Both the good and the bad experiences can be profitable. We humbly thank God for the year that has passed. We can resolve that we will do better in the year to come, enriched by what has passed.

PRAYER FOR THE DAY

I pray that I may carry on with faith, prayer, and hope. I pray that I may carry good things into the year that lies ahead.

Lord, make me an instrument of your peace. Where there is hatred, let me sow love; where there is injury, pardon; where there is discord, union; where there is doubt, faith; where there is despair, hope; where there is darkness, light; where there is sadness, joy.

Grant that I may not so much seek to be consoled as to console; to be understood as to understand; to be loved as to love.

For it is in giving that we receive; it is in pardoning that we are pardoned; and it is in dying that we are born to eternal life.

SAINT FRANCIS OF ASSISI

Notes

Other daily meditation books that will interest you...

Today's Gift

  Today's Gift is our first daily meditation book written with the family in mind. A collection of readings written specifically to help us, as individuals, deal with our family concerns, *Today's Gift* is an excellent companion for those of us involved in A.A., Al-Anon, Alateen, Adult Children of Alcoholics, and other self-help groups. *Today's Gift* will inspire discussion among family members — child and adult alike — and help us all to pause, regain a sense of balance, and recognize the riches we have within and around us. (400 pp.)
Order No. 1031

The Promise of a New Day

  by Karen Casey and Martha Vanceburg

  Written in the tradition of *Each Day a New Beginning,* this guide reaches out to all people who seek full, healthy living. One page at a time, one day at a time, these meditations will guide your path, affirm your strength, and give you hope and peace. Our number three best seller, *The Promise of a New Day* is a fine meditation book for men and women looking for greater rewards in daily life. (400 pp.)
Order No. 1045

For price and order information, please call one of our Customer Service Representatives.

Hazelden ®
Educational Materials

Pleasant Valley Road
Box 176
Center City, MN 55012-0176

(800) 328-9000
(Toll Free. U.S. Only)

(800) 257-0070
(Toll Free. MN Only)

(612) 257-4010
(Alaska and Outside U.S.)